Humbled

in the place of intercession
and spiritual warfare

Carlos Annacondia

Printed by TJ International Ltd, Padstow

Acknowledgements

I would like to express my heartfelt thanks to my wife Maria. She has been, and continues to be, the ideal helper that Jesus has placed by my side. Over many years, while I have been away serving the Lord in evangelism campaigns, she has supported me by her prayers. Several times a year, I would be away from home for between forty and seventy days without a break.

From the headquarters (our home), she built up an altar of prayer and devotion to God, never failing to trust in Him. With nine children, she had quite a task guiding them in their studies, correcting them, training them, while all the while keeping our home spotless. She has always been there to meet me at airports, service stations or in the door of our home, always with a loving smile. She has never complained about the amount of time that I have had to spend away from home.

Although she has often had to stay at home with the family, her heart is for all the wonderful things that the Lord has been doing in the campaigns. She would often pack our kids into the car, and drive thousands of kilometres to enable our family to spend a weekend together during a campaign.

The only reason that I am able to tell about all the wonderful things that God has done as I visit conferences, seminars, or write in magazines and books, is because Jesus has placed my beloved wife as an angel to support me.

Thank you, Maria! You make up more than half the ministry that Jesus gave to us thirty-three years ago.

Thanks also to Moses and Sabrina, my son and daughter-in-law. They have worked tirelessly and persistently to collate the messages that I have given over the years.

To our beloved Saviour, Lord of all, be glory and honour forever!

About the author

Carlos Alberto Annacondia was born in the city of Quilmes, close to the capital city of Buenos Aires in Argentina. He is married to Maria, with whom he has raised a family, comprising nine children and, to date, thirteen grandchildren.

On the 19th of May, 1979, he gave his life to Jesus, and from that time on, a passion for preaching the Gospel has captivated his heart.

Shortly after having given his life to Christ in 1981, he began his ministry as an evangelist, preaching the message of Jesus in the slums of Greater Buenos Aires. He has travelled to many countries, taking with him the message that transformed his life and his family.

The reason for the title of the book

The story begins thirty-three years ago, after I had just received the baptism of the Holy Spirit. Supernaturally, I began to see people's need, and I was filled with a tremendous sense of sorrow and compassion.

The Holy Spirit led me into some times of intense prayer; I would spend a lot of time alone in the presence of God, weeping, and crying out for the needy people that God showed me.

This experience took hold of me and changed my life forever. King David expressed a similar sentiment, when he declared 'I am worn out from my groaning. All night long I flood my bed with weeping and drench my couch with tears' (*Psalm 6:6*).

I can remember those prayer times as though they happened yesterday. Being a new Christian, I didn't understand why those things were happening. I would spend hours kneeling by my bed, weeping and crying out to God, to the point that the sheets were soaked by the time I finished.

That season of praying, weeping and crying out for the needs of the people, went on for quite a long time. As I knelt, humbled, and surrendered in God's presence, He showed me there was something important that I could do for all the needy people. Then I understood the purpose of being humbled and surrendered in God's presence.

The deep humbling that I experienced enabled God to reveal to me His plan for my life and my family. This was something that I could never have imagined or invented. From that place of humility He began to generate a clear purpose that would change the course of this businessman's life forever. The Bible declares:

> If my people, who are called by my name, will humble themselves and pray and seek my face and turn from their wicked ways, then I will hear from heaven, and I will forgive their sin and will heal their land. (*2 Chronicles 7:14*)

What a wonderful truth for this time when we have so much need of an open heaven.

Beloved Church of Jesus Christ, the only way is to be humbled, in surrender before the King of kings. We have to realise that we are nothing, and that we need Him and long for Him. Our desire is to follow in His footsteps, presenting Jesus to a world which is groaning with pain.

Before the world can be touched by God, the Church has to be touched first. For this to occur, we need to learn to be humbled in God's presence.

Carlos Annacondia

Contents

Foreword 1

Introduction 3

1 | The Secret to Revival – Part One 7

2 | The Secret to Revival – Part Two 15

3 | Know Your Enemy 27

4 | The Authority of Satan 37

5 | It is Finished 45

6 | The Gospel Unveiled 57

7 | A Call to Spiritual Maturity 71

Appendix

    Kill the Evangelist 75

    'Mar del Plata, Jesus loves you!' 76

    Testimonies from Campaigns 80

Foreword

In God's book, the Bible, the apostle Paul says the following: 'For I am not ashamed of the gospel, because it is the power of God...' (*Romans 1:16a*). God gives this Gospel of power to all who dare to trust in Him and His Word, and who believe that all that is written in His word is Yes and Amen, for ever and ever.

So this book presents to every man and woman a challenge to believe in the power of God for salvation, deliverance, healing, restoration and victory here on Earth.

God is a god of power and love. He demonstrated this through His Son Jesus Christ, who shed His precious blood for us all, on the cross of Calvary, discarding no one. His love and power reach all who dare to trust and believe in Him.

God wants you to experience each of the testimonies that you read in this book. God has done these things in our lives over the years since we together gave our hearts, our lives and everything that we have to Jesus.

Over the last thirty years, the Lord has never failed us or our family. He remains faithful in every situation that we go through, no matter how difficult it is. We have experienced his love and power in our marriage as God has taught us to forgive each other, understand each other, and love each other. Together with our children, we have been taught and guided to trust Him as we have grown up in the fear and love of the Lord. And when sickness or problems have come, the Lord has shown us each day that the only way to receive His blessings is by trusting in His power, and by holding on to His promises. These are for all his children, who live according to His Word.

May this book be a source of inspiration and blessing for each one of you.

Maria Annacondia

Introduction

I opened my eyes to the world for the first time on the 12th of March, 1944. I was the second of Vicente Annacondia and Zunilda Alonso's three sons. I lived the first years of my childhood and adolescence in a typical home. When I was only ten years old I learned the meaning of the words work and effort, though this was of necessity, not choice.

Once I had matured and found a stable job, I met my wife, Maria, and we decided to get married. Over the years, our family grew. We had our own home, and we were comfortably off compared to other ordinary families. But it was only when I was thirty-five years of age that I really started to live. I had been born thirty-five years previously, but on the 19th of May, 1979, I was born again. This was the date of my spiritual birth when I asked Jesus to come into my life. A week after accepting Jesus as my Saviour, I was baptised by the Holy Spirit.

From that moment on I was filled with a passion for telling the whole world about the Jesus who had transformed my life, my family, and all that I am. This gave new purpose and meaning to my life. Today, thirty-three years later, that same passion continues to fill everything: my life, my dreams, my plans. This amazing call from God has taken me around the world to tell the nations, peoples and languages, about the Jesus who died and rose again for us to give us the victory for eternity.

The Bible teaches us how beautiful and wonderful is this task of evangelism, and its vital importance for our Lord Jesus Christ. When I read the following passage of the Bible, I am reminded of the supreme task we have as the Church, as the body of Christ, to get up and go out to announce, proclaim, and tell everyone that He is the way, the truth and the life:

> He said to them, 'Go into all the world and preach
> the gospel to all creation. Whoever believes and is
> baptised will be saved, but whoever does not believe
> will be condemned. And these signs will accompany
> those who believe: in my name they will drive out
> demons; they will speak in new tongues; they will
> pick up snakes with their hands; and when they
> drink deadly poison, it will not hurt them at all; they
> will place their hands on people who are ill, and they
> will get well.' (*Mark 16:15-18*)

During my thirty-three years of ministry, I have noticed with
sadness how the church throughout this world has often put
this command to one side. For some, the task of evangelism has
become a burden; for others it has become a duty, just another
event in the diary. Thinking of evangelism in this way will lead
to failure.

This is the reason why I decided to write this book: in the
light of God's word, I want to tell you what God has taught me
over the years about the meaning of evangelism.

As the Church of Jesus we must understand that the great
task of evangelism is a call to engage in spiritual warfare. To
put it more simply, evangelism is putting spiritual warfare
into practice. It's going out from the four walls of our church
into the enemy's territory, the place we call the world, into the
squares, parks, streets, to the places where Satan is in control,
where he rules and where he keeps people in slavery to sin. It
means going out from our headquarters, where the soldiers are
prepared for battle, to occupy the enemy's territory. More than
that, evangelism is snatching from the devil's claws the souls
that he has held captive.

The above verses from Mark 16:15-18 give us a clear mission, which combined with the strategy revealed in 2 Corinthians 4:3-4, can be carried out using the tools mentioned in Ephesians 6:10-18. Furthermore, we the Church of Jesus, have the authority to order the devil to loose the souls so that the Gospel can shine in all the Earth.

The Word of God not only gives us the call, it shows us the problem, and offers us the solution. It's up to us to do what the Bible says.

I pray that a passion for evangelism will take hold of your life. May you understand, be conscious of and able to exercise the authority that God has given you to defeat the devil, so that many may come to know Jesus. May you become a Christian who prays passionately for those who have a deep need to know Jesus. Today, more than ever, we need to cry out to God for the needy, and at the same time go out to look for them.

> Lord Jesus, may the words of this book inspire many to take your Word and go out in the authority you have given us to see the results you promised us. Amen.

1

The Secret to Revival – Part One

One day I found myself with the American evangelist Stephen Hill and his wife, and they told me about something they had experienced during a visit to one of our evangelism campaigns in Argentina. One of the reasons this couple had come to Argentina as missionaries was to visit one of our evangelism campaigns. They had heard about the incredible move of God that was happening in Argentina, and they wanted to see for themselves the incredible conversions that had been reported. (Stephen and Jerry Hill were missionaries in southern Argentina for several years. After they returned to the US, the Holy Spirit used them in a revival in Pensacola that touched the whole world.)

One evening, Stephen and his wife visited one of our evangelism campaigns. They hadn't told anyone about their reason for being there, but as they wandered among the crowds, they were approached by someone who asked them rather directly 'Would you like to know the key to the spiritual victory that you can see here?' Their immediate response was 'Of course!'

The person then guided them through the crowd to the back of the large raised platform, from where the Gospel was being preached. Peering under the platform they could see hundreds of people, including my wife, Maria, who were spending many hours in intense intercession, praying, weeping, moaning and crying out to God. As they looked on, their companion, whom they were never to see again, said to Stephen and Jerry 'Here you have the key, the secret to what is happening here.'

From the beginning of our ministry, God showed us that prayer and intense intercession were a vital part of the spiritual victory that He would give us. When I heard this story, the Lord reminded me again of this precious truth.

Much has been said about prayer. We know there are different ways of praying and different types of prayer, but I would like to share with you about intercession.

Intercession is born at the very altar of God, when a believer kneels with a heart that is suffering for lost souls, and from seeing a world without hope that is heading for destruction.

When we look into the Word of God, we find teaching about what true intercession is.

The fire that burns continuously

Leviticus 6:12-13 tells us:

> The fire on the altar must be kept burning; it must not go out. Every morning the priest is to add firewood and arrange the burnt offering on the fire and burn the fat of the fellowship offerings on it. The fire must be kept burning on the altar continuously; it must not go out.

The duty of the priest was to keep the flame lit. 'Every morning' he had to place firewood on the altar. There still is a lighted altar, I'm referring to a personal altar, when we pray for our own needs, for our family, for our country, for our government, for the Church, and for those who are suffering.

This same image is valid for our lives at the present time, even though our ministry is different from the priests of the Old Testament. Each morning we must rekindle the fire on the altar. If we let the fire go out, we will be failing to obey a principle that God teaches us. We must maintain our personal altar, keeping our devotion to God alight. We cannot let it go out for any reason.

Many times the rush and many activities of everyday life mean that our prayer life becomes a duty. We only have time to pray 'Lord, bless this day. Watch over my life and my family. Amen.' But God is looking for something more. Keeping the fire burning involves more work than just coming to the altar.

It is known that fire is one of the main elements in the fight against the impurities, germs and micro-organisms that are harmful to our health. 'Fire kills everything,' they say. The same applies to the fire on the altar: it burns everything. When we place ourselves in front of the altar, in front of the burning flame, the Lord deals with all our impurities.

God is looking for men and women who are prepared to get on their knees before Him, being concerned not only about their own needs, but interceding for those who are suffering. When we do this, our prayer reaches the very throne of God.

As we turn our lives towards God, we must seek to enter his presence, reaching His inner throne room. That is the place where all the army of heaven worships him day and night; in that place there are angels, archangels, cherubim, seraphim and elders. Together with them, we throw ourselves at the feet of Jesus. When we realise in our hearts that we have reached that special place, it is difficult to hold back the tears, knowing with certainty that He is listening to us.

God is looking for priests

The Lord has raised us up to be kings and priests. We have a good understanding of our roles as kings, with all the privileges and benefits that we can enjoy, and the promises on which we can rely. But Revelation 1:6 mentions that there is also a priesthood. This passage says 'and has made us to be a kingdom and priests to serve his God and Father.'

We find it easy to accept that we are reigning with the Lord Jesus, who has placed us at the top, where we can enjoy the riches and blessings of his Kingdom. But what the Lord is searching for in these times is priests, those who are willing not only to enjoy the blessings, but to sacrifice themselves for others; not for them is the applause, because no-one sees what they are doing; and no-one notices when they lose their voice through shouting as they tell the devil to let go of the souls which he holds in bondage.

Our duties, functions, privileges and responsibilities as Christians are two-sided: On the one hand we are kings (as many of us try to be), but on the other hand we are priests. And what is the function of the priest? Very simply, a priest is someone who puts himself between God and man, taking responsibility for the sins of the people. Ezekiel 22:30 puts it this way:

> I looked for someone among them who would build up the wall and stand before me in the gap on behalf of the land so I would not have to destroy it, but I found no one.

God is looking for brave men and women who are prepared to lay down their lives before Him, and who are not content to just enjoy his blessings. In the Scriptures we have many examples of true priests. We find Moses who, on repeated occasions as we read in the following passages, presented himself before God to cry out for his people:

> Moses returned to the LORD and said, 'Why, Lord, why have you brought trouble on this people? Is this why you sent me? Ever since I went to Pharaoh to speak in your name, he has brought trouble on this people, and you have not rescued your people at all.'
> (*Exodus 5:22-23*)

> Then Moses cried out to the LORD, 'What am I to do with these people? They are almost ready to stone me.' (*Exodus 17:4*)

> So Moses went back to the LORD and said, 'Oh, what a great sin these people have committed! They have made themselves gods of gold. But now, please forgive their sin—but if not, then blot me out of the book you have written.' (*Exodus 32:31-32*)

> The people came to Moses and said, 'We sinned when we spoke against the LORD and against you. Pray that the LORD will take the snakes away from us.' So Moses prayed for the people. (*Numbers 21:7*)

When the people were hungry, Moses cried out to God. When the people were thirsty, Moses interceded for them before the Lord. Whenever the Israelites found themselves in trouble and suffering, there was Moses burdened by all the needs of the people, taking responsibility for them before God.

Daniel was another faithful priest for God. Although he himself had not committed the sins of the people, he made them his own as he cried out to God for forgiveness as he fasted, wept and covered himself in ash.

> So I turned to the Lord God and pleaded with him in prayer and petition, in fasting, and in sackcloth and ashes. I prayed to the LORD my God and confessed: 'Lord, the great and awesome God, who keeps his covenant of love with those who love him and keep his commandments, we have sinned and done wrong. We have been wicked and have rebelled; we have turned away from your commands and laws.

> 'Lord, in keeping with all your righteous acts, turn away your anger and your wrath from Jerusalem, your city, your holy hill. Our sins and the iniquities of our

ancestors have made Jerusalem and your people an object of scorn to all those around us. Now, our God, hear the prayers and petitions of your servant. For your sake, Lord, look with favour on your desolate sanctuary.' (*Daniel 9:3-5,16-17*)

And we could talk about many others such as Abraham, Deborah, Jeremiah, Joel, Elijah and other people who placed themselves in the breach, before the Lord, to cry out for others.

The prayer that pleases God

Using a parable, Jesus taught us that although there are many ways to pray, there is one prayer that touches the heart of God.

Two men went up to the temple to pray, one a Pharisee and the other a tax collector. The Pharisee stood by himself and prayed: 'God, I thank you that I am not like other people—robbers, evildoers, adulterers—or even like this tax collector. I fast twice a week and give a tenth of all I get.'

But the tax collector stood at a distance. He would not even look up to heaven, but beat his breast and said, 'God, have mercy on me, a sinner.'

I tell you that this man, rather than the other, went home justified before God. For all those who exalt themselves will be humbled, and those who humble themselves will be exalted. (*Luke 18:10-14*)

Prayer is more than coming before God to bring requests in a carefree and indifferent manner. It's pouring out our hearts before God with tears, knowing that we are nothing before Him. Just like that publican who could only weep and beat his chest, as he cried out for forgiveness.

An intense prayer from the heart is the one that receives

an answer from God. Many times our prayer is just a series of words, something that comes from the mind. But we can only practise deep intercession when we have seen the sufferings of those for whom we are interceding.

How I can pray for a drug addict if I have never seen one dying in a hospital, or never felt for a mother desperately seeking help for her addicted son? We know that when drugs get into a home, they destroy not only the addict which they hold prisoner by the chains of addiction, but also by the pain and suffering caused to other members of the family.

I cannot truly intercede for someone who is a prisoner to alcohol unless I know or have seen the violence that exists in a home where someone is an alcoholic. The whole family suffers violence, aggression and pain from seeing the destruction of their loved one.

When I pray for marriages, for families, the first thing that comes to my mind is what I have seen hundreds of times in campaigns: children crying, tugging at my sleeve, pleading with me to pray that mum or dad would come home, so that they can have a family again. Then I know how to ask, how to pray, how to intercede. It is not difficult for me to groan, because I am visualising the consequences of a broken marriage. I feel the same when I go to a hospital and approach a stretcher to pray for a patient.

We will not be able to intercede unless we sense that cry of pain, that piercing cry of someone who is suffering, unless we can see the agony in their faces as they await death; people who are in agony, crying from the pain of their illness, asking us for help.

If you are willing to intercede, get yourself a large handkerchief because you're going to drench it with tears. When we feel the pain and suffering of others, the least we can do is cry out to God with tears and groans. The Word of God says:

> Those who sow with tears will reap with songs of joy.
> (*Psalm 126:5*)

Some think the secret is in the time spent in prayer. But the number of hours spent repeating words is not what counts. What counts is the way that we pray. I place more value on one or two hours spent crying and groaning in intense prayer than on eight or ten hours spent saying a prayer with which no-one agrees.

The world is groaning. Whom shall I send?

It was in times of intercession that God gave me a vision: I saw before me a jelly-like globe, that was beating like a heart. From the inside of this 'little world' were coming howls, screams of terror, panic, pain, despair, cries of someone who was being raped or was dying; crying and screaming of all kinds. In the middle of all this I heard a voice that said, 'The world is groaning. Whom shall I send?' Three times over I heard the same voice and cry. After I'd heard the voice three times, I remember saying, 'Lord, send me. I'll go.' Of course, I could not imagine what would happen later on. All I said was, 'Lord, send me.'

God still has the same expectation, as he looks for people who are willing to sacrifice their time, not only to preach the Gospel, but also to intercede, to groan, to cry out, and to weep for those who are in need.

The Bible teaches that Jesus himself prayed before the Father in this way:

> During the days of Jesus' life on earth, he offered up prayers and petitions with fervent cries and tears to the one who could save him from death, and he was heard because of his reverent submission. (*Hebrews 5:7*)

Let's take our Saviour as our supreme example and begin to pray, cry out, groan, weep with loud cries and tears for those who are lost. Let's not let a day pass without this being a reality in our lives.

2

The Secret to Revival – Part Two

Over the years, as the Lord has guided us, we have come to realize that the spiritual warfare that so many speak about is not some formula or recipe that can be taught in an academic way. Nor is it a series of steps that we have to learn. Many have taught on this topic, and dozens of books have been written, but the majority talk of what they have heard or think that they know. Many are the methods and strategies that are used to wage the spiritual battle. But the truth is that spiritual warfare begins with intercession. It is something that is only born deep down in a person's heart, after they have seen other people's pain. Then that person can enter into a struggle, not against other people, but against Satan and his army.

Why call it 'spiritual warfare'? When we refer to a war in human terms we mean combat, a battle, a fight, a body to body confrontation. Something similar happens in the spiritual realm.

This is about a battle that we wage against the devil and his army. The only difference with the wars that we know, the sort that occur between nations, is that those ones use all kinds of weapons such as machine guns, rifles, missiles etc, in fact any instrument that can harm the opponent. Our battle does not need physical weapons because as 2 Corinthians 10:4 says: 'The weapons we fight with are not the weapons of the world. On the contrary, they have divine power to demolish strongholds.' Our battle begins with prayer and intense intercession.

Prayer – the key to spiritual warfare

I could tell you many stories about the various spiritual battles that we have had, about the attacks of the devil, and about how the Lord finally gave us the victory when we stopped to intercede and fight against the devil's army.

We know perfectly well that our struggle is not against people nor human institutions. Many times as Christians we get confused and involved in all kinds of arguments. But who is the one who puts a spanner in the works to hold the Church back? It's Satan. Behind people, laws or governments that try to stop the preaching of the Gospel is the devil, Satan. Ephesians 6:12 tells us:

> For we do not wrestle against flesh and blood, but against principalities, against powers, against the rulers of the darkness of this age, against spiritual hosts of wickedness in the heavenly places. (NKJV)

A biblical example of what I am saying is found in the Book of Daniel:

> Then he continued, 'Do not be afraid, Daniel. Since the first day that you set your mind to gain understanding and to humble yourself before your God, your words were heard, and I have come in response to them. But the prince of the Persian kingdom resisted me twenty-one days. Then Michael, one of the chief princes, came to help me, because I was detained there with the king of Persia. Now I have come to explain to you what will happen to your people in the future, for the vision concerns a time yet to come.' (*Daniel 10:12-14*)

Note what the angel said to Daniel: 'But the prince of the Persian kingdom resisted me twenty-one days.' Now a human prince could not resist an angel. So then, what sort of prince is he talking about? He's referring to Satan. The spiritual prince, who was ruling over Persia and who had authority there, was resisting what God had ordered in response to Daniel's need. The same thing happens today; in every city there are principalities and powers which resist the will of God for his children.

If you really want to see victory in your life, you will have to fight against these spirits of unbelief, against these demons which try to stop the blessing of God from reaching his children. But consider how this works: 'Daniel. Since the first day that you set your mind to gain understanding and to humble yourself before your God, your words were heard' (*Daniel 10:12*). 'Set our mind to gain understanding' means feeling first hand the pain and the need of the person for whom we are praying. 'Humble yourself' means to pour out your heart before God as you picture drug addicts being torn apart by the devil, marriages being destroyed, or children abandoned. It means crying, groaning and interceding with tears and pain for those who are suffering. When this happens, God mobilises all his army and begins to break the chains and the barriers of the Devil. We have authority to pray in this way so we can defeat our enemy and take back what Satan has robbed from us.

We need to be aware of the following principle: we have the legal right to claim and take back what the devil has stolen from us. God granted this right to us when He was victorious on the cross of Calvary.

If we fail to gain the victory over these principalities in prayer and intense intercession, then the light of Christ will never shine out. We might have some measure of blessing, but never the great blessing of being victorious, as God desires. We can only defeat our enemy, the devil, by humbling ourselves, weeping, pleading, crying out and commanding: 'Devil, loose the souls that you are holding captive, loose the drug addicts, loose the sinners!' and by engaging in battle in the name of Jesus.

One day, we were in the city of Tucuman with all our equipment that we had brought from Buenos Aires: tents, seating, platforms, lighting, etc. We had a lot of problems with the arrangements. When we arrived at the site that the city council had promised us for our evangelism campaign, a former airport, we were distressed to be told that it was no longer available. The excuse was that it was needed for building a new park, which needless to say was never built. So this is how we found ourselves in Tucuman with all our equipment, but without a venue for our campaign.

A local Christian offered us the use of a site, but it was some way from the city centre, with poor communication and transport links. But since it was the only option that we had, we decided to hold our campaign there. I felt very discouraged by what was happening: the struggle had begun.

Because the site of the campaign was a bit out of the way, we thought we could still reach the people of the city by broadcasting the meetings on local TV, but this request was turned down. Then we planned to do radio broadcasts of the meetings, but this led nowhere, as the networks were asking for enormous sums of money, and they would not even consider our offers. It seemed that all the forces of the enemy were engaged against us. We couldn't get anything organised. All that we had was a field with an uneven surface, which needed to be cleared before we could use it. There were no public transport services to the site. Anyone who decided to come to the campaign would have had to make their own way there, and that was not easy.

We realised that people would not be aware of the campaign unless we could broadcast the meetings by television or radio. When we have a campaign site that is in a prominent place, people who are passing by can see what is happening. That is why we always choose sites close to the city centre, so that people are aware of what is taking place, and can come along if they want to. But it wasn't going to be like that in Tucuman, because the site was completely out of view.

A tremendous spiritual battle ensued. As was our custom in every campaign, we prayed, binding the strong man, the principality over the area. We rebuked the enemy, and in the name of Jesus, we commanded Satan to loose the souls, the homes, the drug addicts, the marriages, the prostitutes, the criminals and all sinners who were in his grip.

We prayed in the same way for the media. Our plan was to have a meeting with media representatives to put forward our proposal. But first, we spent several days in prayer, rebuking the enemy, and commanding Satan to loose the media. We realised that our battle was not against the media bosses, but against the principalities, the powers, rulers of the darkness of this age, and the spiritual hosts of wickedness in the heavenly regions. And for that reason we didn't need to argue with the media bosses.

Humbled, crying out and asking for forgiveness

Once the crusade started, we decided to try again to reach an agreement with the media bosses. It was impossible to pay the sums they were asking for. Our intercession now had a clear objective: 'Lord, touch the hearts of those who are in charge of the media to give us affordable rates, so that the city of Tucuman can hear the Gospel by means of radio and television.' And we kept ordering the devil to loose the media. We had several days of struggle as we engaged in spiritual warfare. They again turned down our offer. They lowered their prices a bit, but it was way more than what we could afford. In the midst of this battle, with the evangelism campaign in progress, some sisters from our ministry, who were praying and interceding for us in Buenos Aires, received a vision from God. In their vision, they saw the city of Tucuman surrounded by flames, which were preventing us from entering. They also noted that the ground inside the circle of flames was coloured red.

Once we heard about this vision, we asked the Lord to show us its meaning. The Lord showed us that the red that was seen on the ground represented the blood of many people that had been shed in the past. The region of Tucuman was the scene of some of the bloodiest fighting that took place during the guerrilla insurgency of the 1970s. We then understood that we had to break the curse over the region arising from this blood that had been shed, and seek God's forgiveness for what had taken place. We decided to gather together Christians who had served in the armed forces during the guerilla war, along with others who had been members of the guerrilla opposition. The various parties from the conflict were represented at our prayer meeting. We came together to seek God's forgiveness, so that the Lord could heal the land, to enable the Gospel to be proclaimed freely.

God heard us, and the result was that the radio and television stations suddenly became available to us. They offered us rates that we could afford, which enabled us to broadcast the evangelism campaign via the TV channels and four radio stations.

It wasn't long before people started coming to the campaign on horseback, in carts, in trucks, in buses, on bicycles and on foot. Around forty thousand people visited the site every day, thanks to what they had seen on television and heard on the radio. When we gave the altar call, people came running to the front. Some seriously ill people were so desperate for help that they were brought along in their bed clothes. The campaign ended up being a tremendous success. Day after day we saw precious souls coming to the feet of Jesus. As captives were set free and powerful miracles occurred, God was glorified.

If we had not engaged in spiritual warfare, but just waited quietly for something to occur, I doubt that anything would have happened. Instead, because we prayed, interceded, rebuked and bound the devil, and the strong man of Tucuman, we were able to see thousands and thousands of people take the decision to follow Jesus during the campaign that went on for forty-five nights.

Gain understanding and humble ourselves before God

We need to gain understanding about the thing we are praying for. We cannot pray in a way that is detached from the situation. The prayers that God desires from us are those which are born deep within, and which come from knowing the pain of those for whom we are praying. When we sense the pain of someone who is suffering, when we feel it first hand, then our intercession changes, and God responds.

A church that doesn't fast or pray, that doesn't weep, is an indifferent church. People will not come to the church unless there is someone there who can beat their chest like the publican, in the parable told by Jesus, as they cry out to the Lord 'God, have mercy on us, for we are sinners.' The spiritual battle must be fought on our knees, groaning and crying out to God with tears and weeping. This is how God will know that we desire to gain understanding and to humble ourselves, just like Daniel humbled himself. He will send his angels to fight for us and to gain us the victory.

The strong man has already been defeated

We also had many struggles in the Argentine city of Santiago del Estero, when we conducted an evangelism campaign there. Even before the campaign began, there had been major problems. We had been given permission to use a strategic location in the centre of the city, and that address had featured in all our advertising for the campaign. This had been going on for some time so that everyone in the city would be well aware of what was going to be happening. All this convinced the state church in the city to stage their own event at the same location, some time before our campaign was due to begin. So a charismatic priest, who believed in miracles and prayed for the sick, came to an event on the site prior to us, and many local people attended. About two weeks before our own campaign was due to begin another priest led a meeting in the same place. But this time it was different. This guy was a parapsychologist, who was quite the opposite of the charismatic priest, who had spoken about miracles. This guy said it was all nonsense, that miracles did not happen, and that the powers of darkness were the products of human imagination.

So there had been quite a spiritual upheaval prior to our arrival. The atmosphere was not at all conducive to carrying out an evangelism campaign. And the local evangelical church, which was quite small in number, was really distressed and concerned about what had happened. From a practical point of view, it seemed that nothing we were planning would be of any impact. However, we decided to go ahead with the campaign.

We had the same struggle with the media that we had experienced in the city of Tucuman. Satan had them under his control, and he didn't want to let them go. While negotiations with the media bosses went on, we kept interceding and demanding that the devil let go of the radio and television. There was no way that they wanted to broadcast the campaign and we were not in a position to pay the price that they were asking. Once again, we began the intercession battle, praying, groaning, weeping and demanding 'Satan, loose the media in the name of Jesus!' We went on like this for several days, morning, afternoon and evening. It was a pitched battle, waged by prayer, and by no other means.

What spiritual warfare is not

At this point I would like to digress and relate an experience to illustrate this point. On one of my trips to Europe, I visited a major city where I met with local believers. As we stood at the front of a church in the city, they told me how they had already implemented many 'spiritual strategies', as they called them, but somehow none of them had worked. Groups of them had circled the city by car as they interceded, they had prayer walked their city; they had prayed in front of the major shrines, statues and monuments, in order to break the covenants that had been made through them; they had even flown over the city, praying from on high. But none of these had made a difference. So when I arrived, the first thing they asked me was: 'Why did none of this work?'

My response was simple: firstly I believe that encircling a city in prayer has been done before, in the city of Jericho, where it was something commanded by God. According to my understanding, it is not the act of encircling a city that brings victory, but the prayers of believers on their knees who are crying out to God with groans, commanding Satan to 'Loose the city, loose those that you are holding captive, the drug addicts, the alcoholics, loose the marriages that you are destroying!' Interceding in this way for those who are suffering is what makes a difference. Encircling a city in prayer doesn't change anything because the battle is not against flesh and blood, but against principalities. Satan has to get his filthy hands off, and loose the people that he is holding captive.

I have already explained to you what needed to be done. I don't want to belittle someone else's strategy, but I believe that intercession is the strategy that is found in the Bible. This is what the priests of God were doing when they placed themselves between God and the people in order to cry out for them. Intercession is what Jesus did in the Garden of Gethsemane, as described in the following passage from the Bible: 'And being in anguish, he prayed more earnestly, and his sweat was like drops of blood falling to the ground' (*Luke 22:44*). During that prayer millions of souls were snatched from the clutches of the devil. Perhaps our own souls included. This is the kind of intercession that is effective, and we must put it into practice.

This was what we did in the city of Santiago del Estero, commanding Satan in the name of Jesus to loose the city, its people and the local media. We started praying early each morning. We were staying in the middle of a residential neighbourhood, and although we tried to keep the noise down, it was impossible to hide from the neighbours the fact that we were interceding and crying out for the city. We couldn't avoid shouting and groaning in prayer as we ordered the devil to get out of the city.

During one of those days of intercession, one of the brothers in our team received a vision. In it he saw Satan seated on a throne, that was shaking and bumping as if an earthquake was taking place. The next day, God gave the same vision for a second time. Two or three days later, we received a different vision during our intercession meeting, and this time I also saw it. I remember seeing a vast army of miniature Roman soldiers, rather like dwarfs, who were running from one side to the other. They were running North, South, East and West, not knowing where to escape. What struck me most was seeing all their weapons scattered on the ground. There were all kinds of weapons: sticks, shields, spears, swords, javelins, all scattered on the ground, with the soldiers running around.

Then I asked the Lord: 'What is all this about?'

Immediately the Holy Spirit responded 'The strong man is bound.'

I asked another question: 'But why are the little soldiers running about? Lord why are they disoriented, not knowing what to do?'

'Because the princes have been bound, and the soldiers can no longer receive orders,' answered the Holy Spirit. This meant that the leaders had lost control of their soldiers, who no longer knew what to do or where to attack.

'And why are the weapons lying on the ground?' I asked again.

'Because they have been defeated, and a defeated army flees and abandons its weapons,' came the reply.

This made sense to me. Because if soldiers flee, taking their weapons with them, they are planning to return to continue the fight. They have not been defeated, and once they have re-armed themselves they will attack again. But the army we saw in the vision had been defeated.

From that moment on, we were able to do radio and television broadcasts of the evangelism campaign, because the media had been set free. People came by the thousands, running to receive Jesus. People who just happened to be passing the campaign site in buses or cars, were touched by the power of God. They would come running in, weeping as they cried out to the Lord for forgiveness.

A few days later, something really strange happened. A large group of people got together to try and oppose what we were doing. They arranged for the statue of a saint to be carried in a procession around the neighbourhood where we were holding the evangelism campaign. As the procession crossed the street in front of the site of our meeting, the four people carrying the statue were knocked to the ground by the power of God, and the statue itself was shattered as it hit the ground. People who had been walking behind the statue in the procession began to scream and experience demonic manifestations. The Lord worked powerfully.

The anointing and power of the Holy Spirit was so powerful that we had to arrange early morning meetings so that everyone could attend. People came from all over the region because they had watched the campaign on TV. The day we started the morning meetings, eight hundred people committed their lives to Jesus for the first time.

The result was that tens of thousands of people came to the feet of Jesus. Spiritual warfare, prayer and intercession are what made the difference. I'm convinced the outcome would have been quite different if we had not engaged the enemy in battle and if we had not taken by faith that which God was giving us. If we had not groaned in prayer, and rebuked the devil, the results would not have been as good. However, God gave us the victory.

So how do we gain the victory? By waging war in battle. As Ephesians 6:12 says 'For we do not wrestle against flesh and blood, but against principalities, against powers, against the rulers of the darkness of this age, against spiritual hosts of wickedness in the heavenly places' (NKJV).

What then is spiritual warfare?

Spiritual warfare works in a specific way. In physical warfare, air attack and bombardment by missiles is essential. In spiritual warfare intercession is what softens up the ground in order to prepare for the invasion. When we intercede, it's like we are sending projectiles which weaken the enemy, so that Satan loses strength, retreats and takes his dirty hands off the city.

In physical warfare, a battle cannot be won by air attack alone. What is required is a landing and ground invasion involving hand to hand combat. In spiritual warfare, the ground offensive begins when the church goes out into the streets to preach the Gospel in the open air, so that everyone can have the opportunity to hear the message of Jesus. Then no-one will be able to say that they haven't heard the message. Not only do we pray, intercede and fire off those spiritual missiles, but we also take the land, as we go from house to house and street to street preaching the Gospel.

During our evangelism campaigns there are two things that we do: in the air we wage spiritual warfare; and on the land we go village to village, city to city, preaching and giving testimony on TV and radio. We do both of these things at the same time. Through doing this, the Lord has blessed our ministry and we have seen thousands of people being converted.

It's not sufficient to only labour in prayer and not go out to evangelize. If all we do is pray, we won't be very successful. Nor will we have success if we go out to evangelize without first engaging in the prayer battle, so that the devil is forced to let go of the souls. Both of these things are needed to achieve victory in the spiritual realm, and to see souls come running to the feet of Jesus.

Spiritual warfare requires both intercession and preaching.

3

Know Your Enemy

> Or suppose a king is about to go to war against
> another king. Won't he first sit down and consider
> whether he is able with ten thousand men to oppose
> the one coming against him with twenty thousand?
> (*Luke 14:31*)

If an army intends to launch an attack, the first thing that
they need to do is to understand exactly who they are facing
and what sort of weapons they are carrying. If it ignores the
capability and armaments of the enemy, then the only thing that
the army will achieve is to lose the battle. This is why so much
money is invested in intelligence gathering, and failure to do this
adequately is likely to prove very costly.

However, Christians often try to ignore the devil, thinking
that in this way they can escape attack, or perhaps they think it
is something they don't need to be concerned about. But he is
our enemy, and we need to know what kind of weapons we are
up against.

Our battle is against the devil and his army. He is our enemy.
Surely that means that we can talk about him. He is a devil who has
been defeated. But the Church still needs to know certain things
about him: what are his aims, why did he come, and what are his
schemes? No child of God should be afraid to talk about Satan's

plans. He needs to be exposed. I have met quite a few people who are even afraid to mention his name, thinking that maybe if they ignore him then they will be out of his reach. The devil has been defeated. It was Jesus who defeated him, and we have been given authority by Him so they we can defeat the devil too; the devil is not going to respect us just because we ignore him.

The Word of God says in John 10:10 that the devil came to steal, kill and destroy. He is our enemy. His sole purpose on this earth is to disturb and destroy completely God's children and God's creation.

Do not be ignorant of the devil's schemes

I am deeply struck by the fact that a large part of the church does not want to hear mention of Satan. They even think 'Let's leave him alone so that he doesn't bother us.' But I'm sorry to tell you that it's not like this, because there is no way that he is going to respect us. I believe it is a serious error to think that if we don't interfere with his plans, then he will not interfere with ours. The very purpose of his existence is to destroy us. The devil will always be out to get us, no matter what our attitude is towards him.

There is a danger of two extremes. One is to glorify the devil and see demons everywhere, the other is just to ignore him. It is dangerous to believe that we are completely immune to his schemes, and that he cannot touch us. He cannot harm us if we remain rooted in the Word of God. That's why the Apostle Paul said that we need to be filled with the Holy Spirit and not give an opening to the devil, so that he cannot gain an entrance into our life: 'and do not give the devil a foothold' (*Ephesians 4:27*).

We need to live in holiness, being rooted in the Word of God, because the devil gets us when we drop our guard. One of his main weapons is to sow fear in the lives of those who are working to expose and confront him. But all those who are standing against him need to know that they have a God-given authority to order him about in Jesus' name.

His schemes to frighten us take many forms and guises, but we need to remember that he is a liar who cannot ignore or disobey the authority of the name of Jesus.

Beelzebul in the tent

I would like to tell you about something that happened on the first night of the evangelism campaign that we did a few years ago in a suburb of Buenos Aires called La Boca. The site of the campaign was just a few hundred metres from the famous stadium of the Boca Juniors football club. We had trained about five hundred volunteers to help us in the deliverance tent.

At the end of the meeting, many people came forward to give their lives to Jesus. As we prayed with them for deliverance, many experienced demonic manifestations, and a huge number of people were taken to the deliverance tent to receive ministry.

Each evening of a campaign, after the Gospel message, we give an altar call for those who would like to invite Jesus into their hearts. We then rebuke the devil, commanding him to loose the souls of those who have committed their lives to the Lord. After praying for healing, for the needs of those present, and for the baptism of the Holy Spirit, we come down from the platform to pray for each person who has come forward, with the laying on of hands. There are usually several thousand people waiting to receive ministry.

This particular evening was no different. I was at the front, praying for people, when suddenly one of the volunteers, who was clearly upset, came running over from the deliverance tent shouting 'Brother Carlos! Brother Carlos! Please come with me quickly!' My immediate response was to ask what had happened and why I had to go in person, because I was busy praying for the many people who were waiting to receive ministry.

From her answer, I realised she was terrified: 'It's Beelzebul! Beelzebul is in the deliverance tent!'

The volunteer was trying to tell me that inside the deliverance tent was a person who was experiencing a demonic manifestation and claiming to be Beelzebul; someone with a grotesque appearance, roaring like a wild animal and threatening all those around him and shouting, 'I am Beelzebul!' She said everyone was terrified, and some had even fled, fearing that they were about to be attacked.

Everyone was asking me for help because no-one had the courage to bind the spirit that was controlling the person.

'Brother, you come and do it because you have the authority!' said the volunteer who had called me, still distraught at what was happening.

So I told her clearly 'Sister. I am not going to do it, because it is not me who has the authority, but those who believe.'

The Bible says in Mark 16:16-18 that these signs will accompany 'those who believe'. If we believe that we have the authority then no devil can stand against us; not even the greatest of the demons, or Satan himself, has authority to refuse or ignore an order given in the name of Jesus.

So I said 'Sister, go back to the tent and tell the volunteers with you to take authority and to command the spirit to leave in the name of Jesus.' The volunteer went off and I continued praying for those gathered in front of the platform. After about ten minutes, I noticed the same volunteer shouting to be heard above the crowd. Only this time was different, and she wasn't asking for help. She ran up to me with her hands in the air, and I could make out a smile of victory on her face.

'It works, brother Carlos, it works!' she told me delightedly. 'We bound Beelzebul in the name of Jesus, just as you told us, and then we commanded him to leave. The guy has been set free. Hallelujah!'

They had managed to bind the demon that was controlling that man, they had got him to renounce all his sins, and then they had commanded the spirit of Beelzebul to leave in the name of Jesus.

The army of Satan

We also need to know that the devil has a large army to help him in his fight against the children of God, in addition to the weapons of ignorance about his existence, which he uses.

Contrary to what many people think, Satan is not disorganised. He was taught according to the doctrine of the angels. We mustn't forget that he was second in command until he rebelled and was expelled from heaven. That means his army is like an ordered military unit, with various ranks who follow the orders of their superiors and respect their authority.

The second part of Ephesians 6:12 shows us this hierarchy or command structure very clearly:

> For we do not wrestle against flesh and blood, but against principalities, against powers, against the rulers of the darkness of this age, against spiritual hosts of wickedness in the heavenly places. (NKJV)

Satan is opposed to the extension of the kingdom of God. He also has a kingdom, the kingdom of darkness. He is the absolute ruler of his kingdom (*Matthew 9:34* ...It is by the prince of demons that he drives out demons...) and the army of darkness (*Psalm 78:49b* '... a band of destroying angels...'). He constantly tours his kingdom throughout the earth (*Job 1:7* 'The LORD said to Satan, "Where have you come from?" Satan answered the LORD, "From roaming throughout the earth, going to and fro on it.'") The Scriptures also refer to him as the prince of this world (*John 12:31b* '...now the prince of this world will be driven out').

In this army there are principalities. The term principality is of Latin origin and means: 'Title or rank of prince; territory or place in submission to the authority of a prince'. It is the highest authority and government in a monarchic state. The prince or principality has power over a nation.

There are also powers. According to the dictionary, a power is 'an authority and dominion that has a specific jurisdiction that has been assigned by a royal authority.' What is the royal authority in this case? It's the power of the devil. Satan, the ruler, orders and directs all activities and operations within the area which has been assigned to him.

There are also rulers of the darkness of this age. The ruler or governor is the head of a province, region or city, corresponding to a rank lower down the hierarchy than power. This governor has authority within a defined area, and governs according to the directives of the power or royal proxy.

Then there are hosts. The hosts are groupings of soldiers in a military campaign. This term is used for those footsoldiers who are fighting for the cause, and who are sent to fight. When the above passage refers to hosts, it is not referring to a senior military rank. Satan's hosts appear to be formations of demons. According to the Bible they are intelligent, but evil beings, without a physical body. Their aim on this earth is to steal, kill and destroy.

Clearly Satan has a strong and united army.

The angel of the Lord defends us

One day, a woman who had been late leaving work, decided to take a taxi to get to her destination on time.

'Where to?' asked the taxi driver

'To the junction of Independence Street and Alvarado.'

'To the evangelism campaign?' asked the driver.

'Yes! Why do you ask? Have you already been there?' asked the woman.

'Yes, I've been along to watch,' replied the driver, 'but the guy who speaks seems a bit of a show-off.'

'Oh. Why do you think that?'

'Well, can you tell me why the evangelist needs to have those five people dressed in white suits who walk across the stage while he's talking to the crowd?'

According to Psalm 34:7 'The angel of the LORD encamps around those who fear him, and he delivers them.' For this reason we don't need to be afraid of what the devil wants to do to us. Satan cannot touch a hair of our head. It is sin, and sin alone, that opens the door to the devil.

We've said that the thief comes to steal, kill and destroy, and that we need to know our enemy. We do not need to be afraid of him, but he is always trying to create problems for us.

Do you know what the devil did during the first evangelism campaign that I did? He wanted to set my car on fire. I was preaching the Gospel, and witches, spiritualists and drug addicts were getting converted; every night, people came running from the street into the campaign site. That's why the devil was seriously upset. So, to try and frighten me away, some people came to the campaign one day with the intention of turning over my car, and then spraying it with alcohol to set it on fire. They thought that if they did this, I wouldn't come back. At the time I was driving a Citroën. But much to their surprise, when they laid hands on my car, they were immediately knocked flat on their backs by the Holy Spirit.

On another occasion, a group of people came to the campaign site early one morning and took all the chairs. The next day, when the meeting was about to start, one of the brothers came running up to me to say that the criminals who had stolen the chairs had just brought them back, because every time they had tried to sit on one, they felt an intense heat that burned their backsides!

God is at work! The Holy Spirit of God is on the earth. And his angels are here to help us.

Sometimes when I am praying I say, 'Lord, send five thousand legions of angels.' People often ask why I do this. Well, it's so that God can do the kind of things that I have been describing, and so that the devil does not make us look stupid. Jesus himself, as he hung on the cross, said that if he wanted to he could ask the Lord to send his angels and they would come to help immediately. Do we not have the same authority?

Do you need help? Ask the Lord to send legions of angels and He will send them. If you are working in a tough neighbourhood, then say, 'Lord, send your angels to help me evangelize this neighbourhood.' Then you will see that the Lord never lets us down.

I will give you authority

Often the devil comes to intimidate me and says things like 'You can't get me.' Sometimes he crosses the platform while I am preaching or praying, to shout at me that I can't touch him. My response is always the same: 'I can't, but the one who is with me certainly can. Hallelujah! Satan get out, in the name of Jesus!' This is the authority that God has given us to do His work.

It's not that I'm especially brave, but each minute of my life I rely on God and trust in His Word that tells me in Luke 10:19:

> I have given you authority to trample on snakes and scorpions and to overcome all the power of the enemy; nothing will harm you.

From the outset of my ministry, I have prayed against the work of witches, faith healers, those involved in the occult, and against all the different cults in Argentina. I remember how in one of our campaigns a senior witch was converted. He told me that once he realised that his work was drying up because of our campaigns, he decided to seek the help of other witches in order to wipe me out, because he was losing followers as they were converted in our campaigns. The news about our campaigns had upset all those servants of Satan who were involved in the kingdom of darkness. So he had contacted other witches in Brazil, Paraguay, Bolivia and as far away as France, where witches were aware of the trouble we were causing them. So they had agreed together to do some work of witchcraft in order to put me out of business.

But once this witch was converted, he immediately came to tell me what he had done.

'Brother Carlos, the witches of Brazil, Uruguay, Paraguay and Bolivia say that they are going to destroy you!'

At that moment I felt a chill run down my spine from the top of my head to the tip of my toes: I was afraid. But immediately, I heard a voice in my ear telling me:

'Carlos, I have given you authority to overcome all the work of the enemy, and nothing will harm you.'

Hallelujah! He who is in us is greater than he who is in the world.

4

The Authority of Satan

1 Peter 5:8 says:

> Be alert and of sober mind. Your enemy the devil
> prowls around like a roaring lion looking for someone
> to devour.

So we know that Satan never gives up trying to destroy us. Day
and night he focuses all his energies on making our lives miserable.
All his forces are working with the sole purpose of destroying
God's creation. There is nothing that is more important to him.
The devil's work does not depend on whether we believe in him
or not. In fact, the greatest deception of recent times is denying
that the devil really exists. He is a liar and the father of lies, and
denying his existence is an advantage for him, because when he
is ignored he has greater freedom to attack us. Ignoring him will
not cause us to remain out of his sight. He shows no mercy. It
does not matter to him if we try to ignore him. Even if we don't
mention his name, he still prowls around like a roaring lion,
looking for someone to devour.

I do not preach the devil; I preach Christ. I speak about the
Lord, his love, his blessings. But when I teach, I teach about our
enemy the devil. We need to know not only about the power
that we have to confront the devil, but also about the authority
that he has. And the exercise of our authority requires that we
understand how the devil operates.

To which kingdom do you belong?

Let's look for a moment at what the apostle John says in 1 John 5:19: 'We know that we are children of God.' He wants to open our eyes to the spiritual reality that we belong to God, who is with us; His angels are around us day and night to keep us safe. We know that we have been called by God, and that our lives are in His hands. But the above verse goes on to say, 'and that the whole world is under the control of the evil one.' So we can conclude that many people belong to the Lord. But how many do not belong to Him? Many, many more. Jesus expressed this very clearly in Matthew 12:30 when he said: 'Whoever is not with me is against me, and whoever does not gather with me scatters'. This is absolutely black and white, clear as crystal. There are no grey areas. There is one side or the other. We either belong to the kingdom of God or we belong to the kingdom of Satan.

I frequently hear people say things like: 'He's not a Christian, but he's a good person.' I am sorry to tell you that no matter how good a person may be, if they do not belong to Christ, then they are under the control of the evil one. We all sin, even good people: the famous whom we admire; kings and their subjects; governments and those whom they govern; and astronauts, Nobel Prize winners, artists and football players. Those who come to Christ in faith and repentance have their sins taken away and are reconciled to God through Jesus. Then they belong to God and are part of His Kingdom. But those who have not taken this decision, sadly remain under the control of the evil one. At some point the devil will use these people's lives because they belong to him; they are under his authority and he is their father.

So how important is all this? It is even more important that we can imagine. How much authority does the devil have that he can have the whole world under his feet? In order to understand this, we must explain it from the beginning.

What then is the authority of Satan?

The first part of the answer to this question is found in Luke 4:5-8 which says:

> The devil led him up to a high place and showed him in an instant all the kingdoms of the world. And he said to him, 'I will give you all their authority and splendour; it has been given to me, and I can give it to anyone I want to. If you worship me, it will all be yours.' Jesus answered, 'It is written: "Worship the Lord your God and serve him only".'

The first time I read this passage, it had a big impact on me. I could not understand what was written. It really troubled me. My main problem was with the devil's statement that 'I will give you all their authority and splendour; it has been given to me, and I can give it to anyone I want to.' I immediately asked the Lord how it was possible that Satan could have so much authority unless God had given it to him. I couldn't understand who could have given him authority, so that he could tell the Lord that he was the one who would decide to whom he would give the kingdoms and the authority over all the earth. Did all this really belong to Satan, I wondered. How could Satan wield such authority? I also noted that Jesus did not answer him by saying 'You are lying.' Instead Jesus quoted the word of God, saying 'It is written: "Worship the Lord your God and serve him only."' I felt very confused, because I could not understand what authority Satan has on the earth.

As I searched for an answer, the Lord directed me to different passages of Scripture which speak of Satan as 'the god of this age' and 'the powers of this dark world.' Then I began to see that the Lord recognises that the devil has acquired an authority. I also realised that 'all the kingdoms of the earth' means the whole world; all the nations of the world, with no country excluded.

It's really hard to understand the scale of the authority the devil has over all the nations of the earth. Many times it is easier to talk about other subjects, but it is important to understand what has really happened.

As I became interested, I asked the Lord how it was that Satan had managed to get such authority if it had not been granted to him by Jesus. I asked the Lord to give me understanding from His Word. I knew very well that it was not God who had given him such authority, because He made all the kingdoms of this earth for man and not for the devil. He created the earth and adorned it with all His splendour. Our minds cannot fathom the wonders of God's creation.

In the beginning, the earth was without form and empty, but God brought order by the work of His hands and filled what was empty. For what purpose? So that the devil, the thief and murderer could destroy the work of God's hands? No! God created the earth for us and for our enjoyment. After He had finished adorning the earth by creating trees, plants, flowers, birds, beasts of the field and stunning landscapes, the Lord took mud in His hands and made man, and set him as ruler over all creation, saying: 'Be fruitful and increase in number; fill the earth and subdue it. Rule over the fish in the sea and the birds in the sky and over every living creature that moves on the ground' (*Genesis 1:28*). It's like when parents prepare the home for the birthday of one of their children. They put up streamers and balloons, and decorate everything to make the child feel happy. God's love for us is so great that He has adorned the earth and crowned it by placing us in the midst of it, saying 'All this I have done for you to enjoy.'

God did not create us to live broken lives, full of problems, difficulties, bitterness and sadness. I already understood this full well, but what I didn't understand was who was the one who gave authority over the nations of the earth to Satan.

God's covenant with Adam and with Noah

One day, God led me to read the following verse from the book of Genesis. As the Holy Spirit taught me, for the first time I understood the challenge that Satan gave to Jesus in the desert.

> God blessed them, and said to them [Adam and Eve],
> 'Be fruitful and increase in number; fill the earth and
> subdue it. Rule over the fish in the sea and the birds
> in the sky and over every living creature that moves
> on the ground.' (*Genesis 1:28*)

What was God doing with Adam and Eve? God was crowning mankind with a covenant. I can picture God taking Adam and Eve by the shoulder and walking with them in the light of day. God was giving them the keys and the title deeds to the earth. He commanded them to 'subdue it' and 'rule over', meaning 'to take control of something, and give orders as its owner.'

In other words, God was saying to Adam and Eve 'You can do what you want, steward the earth, manage it, and be masters of the creation.' Nobody had more authority than them. They could do as they pleased, without having to ask or consult anyone. To Adam and Eve God gave complete authority and dominion of the earth, saying 'Rule over it and subdue it.'

Then in Genesis 9:1-2, we find another covenant which God made, this time with Noah and his sons:

> Then God blessed Noah and his sons, saying to them,
> 'Be fruitful and increase in number and fill the earth.
> The fear and dread of you will fall on all the beasts
> of the earth, and on all the birds in the sky, on every
> creature that moves along the ground, and on all the
> fish in the sea; they are given into your hands.'

When we compare these two covenants, we see that there is a

difference between them. It's a very important difference. The covenant that God made with Noah was not the same as the one that He made with Adam and Eve. In this new covenant the basic command to 'subdue it' was not included. This shows that mankind no longer had the authority that it had in the beginning. What could be the reason for the difference? What had happened between the time that these two covenants were made?

The crown has fallen from our heads

Something very important had happened, something that changed the whole course of human life. The reason for the difference is stated very clearly in Genesis chapter 3, which describes the fall of mankind through rebellion and disobedience; Satan defeating Adam and Eve in the Garden of Eden. I can just picture Adam and Eve as they were being expelled from the garden, looking back in desperation and seeing the angel with its sword drawn, blocking their return. That was the moment that sin took hold of them. And that sin did much more than deprive mankind of life in a garden, where all was happy and where they could walk with God himself. In Lamentations 5:16 it is written: 'The crown has fallen from our head. Woe to us, for we have sinned!' Satan triumphed because of the disobedience of mankind, snatching the keys and title deeds to the earth, and usurping the crown given to mankind.

Through his disobedience to God, the first man gave to Satan what God had placed in his hands.

In the wars of old, when one king was triumphant in battle against another, it was not enough for him to simply be the victor. His victory meant much more than merely emerging the winner. Everything that had until then belonged to his opponent, passed legally into the hands of the victorious king;

all their possessions, properties and territories would come under the authority of the victor. The people who were conquered lost all authority. Being conquered meant slavery and subjection to a new kingdom.

Not only did mankind lose all that God had placed into their hands; through sin they became slaves of Satan, belonging to his kingdom. This was how the devil was able to come before Jesus in the desert and challenge Him by saying 'I will give you all their (all the kingdoms of the earth) authority and splendour; it has been given to me.'

Who then was guilty of surrendering to Satan authority over all the kingdoms of the earth? Mankind. We were guilty. Because of our disobedience, God's creation finds itself enslaved by sin, destruction, death, violence, drugs and promiscuity.

You might be wondering why I mention us, and not just Adam and Eve, when I refer to who is responsible for this state of affairs. Well, there's a reason. Before I became a Christian, if someone told me about Adam and about sin, my immediate response was 'How am I to blame for what a man did, who had nothing to do with me, and who lived many thousands of years ago?' I believed that if God was good, then he would not hold me responsible for something that Adam did. That was my excuse, because I didn't know what the Scriptures say.

The Bible says the curse that is on God's creation is a result of Adam's sin. Because of the sin of one man, evil entered the world. It doesn't matter how good we are, or try to be. We are as guilty as Adam. Romans 5:12 states it like this:

> Therefore, just as sin entered the world through one man, and death through sin, and in this way death came to all people, because all sinned.

But praise God that this is not the end of the story, because the same passage of Scripture continues:

> For if the many died by the trespass of the one man,
> how much more did God's grace and the gift that
> came by the grace of the one man, Jesus Christ,
> overflow to the many! (*Romans 5:15*)

It is true that Satan won a legal right over mankind. He was not lying to Jesus when he tempted Him, nor had he taken by force what had belonged to Adam. No, it was given to him. He became master and owner of all that the Lord had made. But Jesus did what Adam could not do to recover what had been lost. He came to pay the debt that we all had with God.

The debt is paid

The day that Jesus Christ came into my life, I understood for the first time the immensity of what He did on the cross. On the 19th of May, 1979, my wife and I decided to give our lives to the Lord. As we said that first prayer that completely change our lives, with tears streaming down our faces, God showed me a vision. My hands were raised in surrender and commitment to Jesus, and I could see Him placing a piece of paper in my hands. It was a receipt on which was written: 'Father, the debt that Carlos had with you is now settled. I've paid it.' And below it was a name. It was signed by Jesus himself, but not in the same ink as the rest of the note. It was signed in His own blood, the blood of Jesus, shed on the cross of Calvary.

Jesus settled the debt that we had with God, and in the process took back all that mankind had lost.

5

It is Finished

> When he had received the drink, Jesus said, 'It is finished.' With that, he bowed his head and gave up his spirit. (*John 19:30*)

There are no words in history so loaded with power and victory as those that Jesus uttered, seconds before giving up his life: 'It is finished.'

Let me explain this a little bit more. When Jesus died on the cross of Calvary, after having been exposed to public humiliation, and having taken on himself the sins of us all, he made a visit to an unexpected place; he descended into hell itself.

In that dark place, Satan and all his company were engaged in a tremendous celebration that they believed would continue for eternity, as they proclaimed 'We won! We have defeated the Son of God!'

Death himself was ready to enslave Jesus for ever and ever. But great was his surprise, when at the very time he did not expect it, the gates of hell were suddenly wrenched open.

Nobody present at that party expected Jesus to arrive, the very one that they had eliminated a few hours earlier. His death was the very reason they were celebrating.

The demons had expected His appearance to be that of a slave to death, but when He entered, His steps were those of the King of kings and Lord of lords.

All hell froze before such authority. The party was over in a second. No one dared to utter even a single word or make any sound. Jesus, with His penetrating gaze of authority, stood facing death himself. With the voice of one who emerges the victor in battle, He proclaimed these precious and unforgettable words: 'Where, O death, is your victory? Where, O death, is your sting?' (*1 Corinthians 15:55*). The one who controlled the kingdom of the dead had lost his authority.

The Bible tells us that the wages of sin is death (*Romans 6:23*). But death could not hold Jesus, because He had no sin.

Now He was defeating and humiliating hell in its entirety. Jesus, the conquering king, was taking from Satan what he had robbed from mankind at the beginning of creation: the keys and the title deeds to the earth.

But that was not all. When He ascended from hell as the victorious king, having accomplished His mission, He displayed to all Heaven what He was carrying in His hands: on His left, the keys and title deeds to the Earth; in His right hand, reconciliation between God and mankind.

Hallelujah! Jesus recovered what mankind had lost in the Garden of Eden.

The scale of the redemptive work of Jesus

What I have just related enables us to understand clearly the significance of what Jesus did that precious day on the cross of Calvary. The Bible tells us in 1 Corinthians 15:22: 'For as in Adam all die, so in Christ all will be made alive.' Jesus reversed the condition of mankind. From the time of Adam till the day when Jesus gave up his life, mankind was in bondage to Satan because of sin. After they were expelled from the Garden of Eden, mankind lost all its privileges. The greatest privilege was walking with God. After sinning, there was no possibility for humans to enter into the presence of God, except through sacrifices. Satan made sure to rob Adam of something he knew was the key to living a life full of peace and happiness; having communion with God, by walking together with Him and talking face to face with his Creator.

From this we can see the value of what Jesus won back for us. He raised us to our original status. His sacrifice restored to us the incredible privilege of being able to walk again with God, at all times and in all places, just as Adam and Eve did in the beginning.

We need to grasp this truth: God is with us. There are no longer any barriers that separate us from God. There are no impediments, and nothing and nobody can hinder our fellowship with God. We can talk to Him any time and any place. We can rely on Him wherever we are. Jesus took away all that separated us from God. Now, through Jesus, the way is open for all. Let's enter in by this way to live a victorious life.

The authority of the Church

One of the wonderful things that Jesus took back from the devil, made possible by His sacrifice on the Cross, is the authority that had been stolen. That authority now belongs to the Church. All who believe, who are children of God and who walk hand in hand together with Him, are the rightful owners of this precious authority. Jesus recovered what we had lost because of our sin, and entrusted it to His Church.

The authority that the Church, the body of Christ, has received is much greater than we can imagine. Not even hell itself can stand against it. This was what Jesus said in Matthew 16:18:

> And I tell you that you are Peter, and on this rock I will build my church, and the gates of Hades will not overcome it.

In the unity of the body of Christ is found the highest authority to overcome the kingdom of darkness. By praying in agreement we can place in subjection any spiritual force in the spiritual realm that is affecting the physical world. We have authority to bind the devil and all his cohorts, and to release abundant blessings and the wonders of God on our lives:

> Truly I tell you, whatever you bind on earth will be bound in heaven, and whatever you loose on earth will be loosed in heaven. Again, truly I tell you that if two of you on earth agree about anything they ask for, it will be done for them by my Father in heaven. For where two or three gather in my name, there am I with them. (*Matthew 18:18-20*)

As the Church of Jesus Christ, we must believe that there are no limits to the exercise of this authority. Those who are children of God by faith need to take hold of it, in order to live a life of victory. Those of us who believe, and who live according to the will of God and what His Word teaches, have authority to overcome temptation and to defeat the devil in all areas of our lives: in our marriage, among our children, at work, in our studies, with our health. We can live a life of complete victory. As James 4:7 says: 'Submit yourselves, then, to God. Resist the devil, and he will flee from you.'

So then, we know that we have received spiritual authority, which should be reflected firstly in our lives. But, as with all things of God, what we have received is not only for personal benefit.

As children of God we have a responsibility. Everyone needs to ask themselves the following question. 'What is the purpose of this authority that I have received? What is my responsibility as a child of God?'

The purpose of the authority we have

The Lord has anointed us, and given us an authority which comes with a purpose. The Bible clearly states in the book of

Isaiah that this is for preaching the good news, binding up the wounded, and proclaiming freedom to the captives:

> The Spirit of the Sovereign LORD is on me,
> because the LORD has anointed me
> to proclaim good news to the poor.
> He has sent me to bind up the broken-hearted,
> to proclaim freedom for the captives
> and release from darkness for the prisoners.
> (*Isaiah 61:1*)

On various occasions, Jesus showed us that we have authority, and He also taught us what we should use it for. When He commissioned the twelve disciples, He told them:

> Heal those who are ill, raise the dead, cleanse those who have leprosy, drive out demons. Freely you have received; freely give. (*Matthew 10:8*)

In the Gospel of Luke 10:19, Jesus instructed the seventy-two as follows:

> I have given you authority to trample on snakes and scorpions and to overcome all the power of the enemy; nothing will harm you.

And then there is the most important of all the commands that Jesus gave us: the Great Commission. It summarizes the authority that Jesus has given us:

> He said to them, 'Go into all the world and preach the gospel to all creation. Whoever believes and is baptised will be saved, but whoever does not believe will be condemned. And these signs will accompany those who believe: in my name they will drive out demons; they will speak in new tongues; they will pick up snakes with their hands; and when they drink deadly poison, it will not hurt them at all; they

> will place their hands on people who are ill, and they
> will get well.' (*Mark 16:15-18*)

Jesus gave us this authority so that we could exercise it on behalf of the needy.

Authority needs to be tested

One morning, as I was reading the newspaper, I came across a report about a town in Patagonia, in the south of Argentina. It was about the city of Las Heras, in the province of Santa Cruz. This small town has a population of about nine thousand. It is a very cold place, with strong winds and a semi-desert climate. It's not a place for tourists and the only people who live there are workers in the oil industry. At that time there was a confrontation between a group of oil workers and the town council. Things came to a head with a man was killed in a clash between an armed group and the local police.

As I read this distressing news, God spoke to me about visiting the town to do an evangelism campaign as soon as possible. We immediately got in touch with the churches and the pastors of the region. After discussions with them about the situation, we made arrangements to hold a campaign. The town council were helpful and offered us a hall to hold our meetings.

God did powerful miracles and many were healed. Members of the town council also came along to hear the message about Jesus. As the Holy Spirit touched people's hearts, we watched as people who had been trying to kill each other just a few days before, were reconciled to each other. Most of the people of the town came to our meetings, and there was a wonderful atmosphere of peace.

I remember very clearly something that happened on the third night of the four-day campaign. After the message, we had given the altar call, prayed for deliverance and for the sick and then listened to some of the wonderful testimonies. I came down from the platform to minister to those who had come forward, when suddenly I was confronted with a terrible sight. Waiting in line with the others, was a giant of a man of about thirty years of age. When I went to pray for him, he grunted in a grotesque voice.

'What have you come to do?'

The Holy Spirit showed me that it was the strong man of that city who was speaking to me. He was not pleased with what we were doing, and had come to get us. Immediately I could feel my body start to tremble. Although I was standing still, the muscles in my face were twitching, and my arms and legs were shaking. It was the first time I had experienced such a situation. However, at no time did fear take over. I understood that the demonic presence in that man was so strong that it was causing all my muscles to shake.

Immediately, I raised my head to look into his eyes. In that instance, for the first time in my life, I saw the very face of Satan. Those who were around me had the same experience. The man reacted by taking about ten paces backwards, leaving me alone with a few helpers, who were waiting for me to tell them what to do.

Then I went up to the spirit and gave the command: 'Satan, in the name of Jesus, I bind you!'

With the authority of the Lord, I then ordered the man to lower his arms, which were raised and poised ready to strangle me. He remained immobile, in the position in which I had bound him, with his hands by his sides, but he continued to roar and shake.

I left him like that and went on with the task of praying for other people gathered at the altar. During all this time the man stood motionless, waiting for the next order that I would give.

I observed many strange things as he waited. Some moved away from him, fearing that perhaps the devil would attack them. Others, including pastors, did not dare go near him, for fear that the spirit might seize them. But from my experience of ministering deliverance over thirty years, I can assure you that there is no way that could happen. Never ever have we had the experience of seeing a demon exit one person and then enter another. So no one needs to be afraid that this could happen. Sin is the only key that Satan has to gain access to a person's life.

During that half hour, everyone was able to see that even the strong man of city, with various principalities under his control, had to submit and could do nothing but obey the commands given him in the name of Jesus. My message that night had referred to the authority the children of God have over the kingdom of darkness. God had illustrated my preaching through what had happened.

When I finished praying for all the people who were waiting, I went over to the man once again and gave the following order to the devil: 'Satan, in the name of Jesus, I command you to leave this person, right now!'

Instantly, he collapsed heavily to the ground, and then opened his eyes. He gave a big smile of relief and freedom. He stood to his feet, and with his hands held high, he gave glory to God. Satan had let him go! Hallelujah!

Through this experience, God gave me another lesson. The authority of His children will be tested, so that they demonstrate that they believe in what has been entrusted to them. The story would not have ended well if I had not believed that I had authority in the name of Jesus. That man, who was under the influence of the devil, would probably have beaten me black and blue. But what I realised very clearly at the time, was that I had an authority. It was not a human authority, but one given me in the name of Jesus, and without which I would not have been able to confront that spirit. And this same authority has been given to the Church by Jesus Christ. If you believe, then you too have this authority.

The people who minister in the deliverance tent are not leaders, pastors, or people with a special calling or gifting. They are members of the churches which have come together to organise the campaign. We teach them the meaning of authority. I can assure you that by the time each campaign ends, each one of them has proved that this authority is effective, because the Lord gives authority to those who believe, irrespective of their age or title.

I can attest to this, because when I had been a Christian for only a few months, and knowing very little, I believed God, and things started to happen. All I had was faith. And that was enough for the authority of God to operate, and the signs started to appear.

Authority is for all who believe

Contrary to what many people think, spiritual authority is not something unique to a person. It's not a special gift or ministry. Nor is it something extraordinary and supernatural that we only see on special occasions. Jesus has made it possible for every believer to experience His authority all the days of their lives. Authority is something that should be part of everyday life, to be used as and when it is necessary.

You need to know that you have authority in order to confront the kingdom of darkness, which is the devil and all his forces. This is what happens when we believe and take authority in the name of Jesus.

Many ask me if deliverance is a specific ministry. Jesus didn't teach that. He said in the Gospel of Mark 16:17: 'and these signs will accompany those who believe: in my name they will drive out demons.' There are no limits; for all who believe, trust, and are seeking God's perfect will for their lives, have power and authority. Obviously, there are certain conditions. We cannot live according to our own way of thinking, without consulting the will of God, and pretend to exercise dominion over the spiritual world. The Bible teaches us how we should live and behave in order to have authority. And no one can have it, unless they first put themselves under that authority.

If we live under authority, Satan has to submit to our commands. However, if there is sin in our lives, what authority can we expect to have to overcome the devil? We have to be careful, otherwise the same thing might happen to us as happened to the seven sons of Sceva, as described in the Book of Acts 19:13-16. The demons will not respect our commands, and they are the ones who will exercise authority over our lives.

From priestess of darkness to servant of Jesus

I remember one night ministering at an evangelism campaign that was taking place close to an area where there was a lot of witchcraft, magic, spiritualism, Voodoo and all kinds of occultic activity. That evening, a vast woman of grotesque appearance came forward to receive ministry. I noticed that there was no hair on her head, which was covered with a scarf. As soon as she approached me, and before I had time to lay hands on her, she began to shake. Immediately, two of the volunteers who were at my side, seeing her advance in fury towards me, tried to restrain her. When I took authority over the spirit that was controlling the woman, the two volunteers put their arms around me to push me back, thinking that in this way they could save me from being attacked. But over the years, I've come to understand, as God has taught me, that spiritual authority does not work in this way. When one person takes authority, the others need to keep still, not talking or interfering. When a person experiences a demonic manifestation during a church service, it can often happen that those who are standing nearby start to pray, shout and rebuke the spirits. But the devil doesn't obey any of them because he respects authority. When a situation like this occurs, deliverance becomes ineffective because each person takes away the other's authority.

Then, while the volunteers were trying to defend me, the woman gave me a slap and her fingernails just caught the edge of my lips. I had to ask the volunteers to let me go, because I didn't need any form of protection. I knew full well that in the name of Jesus, the devil cannot touch even a single hair of my head.

So I went up to the woman and bound the spirit in the name of Jesus. Just then, the Holy Spirit showed me that she was a witch. So I lent over and spoke into her ear 'In the name of Jesus, if you do not repent now, then this will be the last day of your life, because God will take you.'

As I said those words, the woman fell to the ground, as though she had been struck down. My next thought was 'Lord, how can it happen so quickly?' She was then carried off to the deliverance tent by four volunteers, and I lost track of her.

If someone experiences a demonic manifestation during one of our campaigns, the ushers accompany the person to the deliverance area, usually a tent. We do not attempt to minister to the person in public. We believe it is important to respect a person's privacy, and not expose them to the embarrassment of being observed. In the privacy of the tent, the person can confess and renounce the sins that have kept them bound, and so find deliverance.

This woman had a lot to confess because she was a high-level witch. She had made many demonic covenants, and had a large group of personal followers. She spent several hours in the tent receiving ministry, but after the campaign I heard nothing more from her.

Much to my surprise, the next time we organised a campaign in the area, a well-dressed and elegant woman came forward to give testimony, this time sporting a full head of hair. Although she had been transformed completely, I still recognised her as the woman who had confronted me that night. She told the crowds that on the same night that she was touched by the Holy Spirit and set free from the demonic bonds in her life, she was healed of a disease that had been eating away at her life; she had been suffering from cancer. But God in His mercy gave her a second chance and turned her into a new woman. He set her free from all the chains, sadness and bitterness that had dominated her life, and healed her of that terrible disease. In the deliverance tent, she had renounced all the demonic covenants she had made, and occult practices that she had been involved in. She had promised Jesus that from that day forth she would no longer be a priestess of the devil, but a servant of Jesus Christ.

Authority for deliverance

God has given us the same power that he gave to the twelve disciples and to the seventy-two that Jesus sent out. What should we do while all the time the sick are dying, the devil is destroying families, and people are committing suicide?

How sad it would be if God did not break the bonds that keep people bound, oppressed, and under the control of the devil, with no one to do anything for them. But thanks be to God that Jesus Christ, who has compassion for all those who suffer, has given us authority and power, and told us: 'These signs will follow those who believe: In My name they will drive out the demons that oppress, that keep people bound, and which destroy the lives of those He has created.'

God will create opportunities for us to put into practice what we have received. We also have the power to drive out demons, and to exercise authority over the spiritual world. So we need to be wise, and to live lives worthy of the Lord, using the authority He has given us to do His will.

6

The Gospel Unveiled

Satan's headquarters

The following conversation has been adapted from the book *Passion for Souls* by Oswald Smith.

One evening, the rulers of the different regions met at Satan's headquarters to give an update on developments in the territories under their control.

'Right, what's the news?' Satan asked, as he lifted his head and stared questioningly at the assembled group.

'Good news, sir!' replied the ruler of Region One. 'They have been unable to achieve their aim.'

'So they tried then?' responded Satan, as he looked into the face of the fallen angel.

'Yes, my Lord, but to no avail. All their efforts were frustrated.' replied the ruler as he bowed, looking very pleased at his recent victory.

'So how did it go? Did you have a lot of work? Tell me all about it!' demanded Satan, keen to know more.

'Well,' began the ruler, 'as I was wandering through the territory under my command, I overheard a pastor saying that they were about to hold a meeting for all the pastors in the city to discuss the possibility of arranging an evangelism campaign.'

'Just tell me what you did,' Satan interrupted, impatient to hear the end of the story.

'Firstly, I called together all the forces of darkness under my command for a meeting. They made many suggestions, but we finally agreed that the best scheme was to prevent them from working together. That was really easy to do. All we had to do was to remind the pastors that some of those coming to the meeting had split away from existing congregations. We sowed feelings of bitterness and resentment. But that's not all. We also brought to light some sins from the past, thanks to critical comments about the pastors that we picked up from church members when they changed from one congregation to another. We sowed plenty of thoughts of jealousy and envy. With others, we used an even simpler strategy. All we had to do was remind them that there were some doctrinal differences between the various pastors who had gathered. It was quite simple to make them lose sight of their objective. Finally, all we had to do was release among them a spirit of strife and division. That was the finishing touch that ended any plan of working together. Now they are more disunited than ever. Our work was a complete success. I can say that everything is in order in my territory.'

'Excellent! Great work! You have done me a great service,' said the fallen cherub, with an expression of satisfaction on his face, which once had been beautiful.

Shouts and applause echoed through that dark and awful place.

'Continue your good work, ruler of Region One. Keep killing and destroying everything in your path, including the youth, marriages, the elderly, and children. Keep using drugs, alcohol, sex and violence to ruin the region under your control. It looks like you should have no problems.'

Then he turned to the ruler of the Region Two and enquired, 'Well, what have you to report?'

'I've also got some great news that will make your Majesty really happy,' said the ruler.

'Oh. Has there been an attempt to invade your region?' Satan asked, with growing interest.

'Indeed there was,' replied the ruler. 'I was carrying out my duties in the territory under my command, a region where there are very few churches. I was busy destroying congregations, dividing them, preventing the raising up of new servants of that unmentionable person (Jesus), when I heard the news that some new missionaries were going to be coming to my region from another country. I quickly called a meeting of the forces under my command, and we soon came up with a plan, which we carried out with great success. We sent a strong spirit of sickness to oppress the missionaries. They soon gave up their call, thinking that they had made a mistake, and that perhaps preaching the Gospel was not so important after all.'

'And that is not all, my Lord,' continued the ruler. 'We used people under our control to put up the rental costs of the buildings where Christians have been meeting. Now they have decided to leave our area for good.'

As he concluded his report, a great shout of joy went from the assembled rulers who bowed before the majestic figure of Satan.

'And what have you got to report?' he asked, turning to another fallen angel. 'Are you still the master of Region Three?'

'I'm afraid that my news is not good, my Lord,' responded the ruler, slowly, with a look of terror, without looking up.

'What!' thundered Satan, barely able to control himself. 'Have you not been able to keep your region under control?'

'We did our best, your Majesty, but to no avail.'

'Are you so useless that you couldn't even stop an evangelism campaign?' roared the boss, mad with anger.

'Not only were our attempts to stop it unsuccessful, but the campaign went on for longer than scheduled. They've been preaching the Gospel every night for forty days. Thousands have heard the message and many have been healed. My Lord, it's a disaster! There are even pastors and entire congregations coming to help from other areas. Even our supporters, the witches, are being converted. Your majesty, it's a complete failure.'

'But that's not possible! I sent entire legions to support, and you still couldn't stop it!' thundered Satan.

He then broke into an uncontrollable rage. The air was filled with millions of spirits. Their rulers were seated in front of Satan, terrified, as they struggled to avoid his piercing gaze. The entire assembly sat in rapt attention.

Then the ruler stepped slowly forward, crestfallen, until he stood trembling before his sovereign.

'There was no way that we could stop them. Our forces worked day and night trying to beat them, but the heavenly army was more numerous than ours. Their Father sent many legions of angels to protect them and defeated us on all fronts. It seems they have started an organisation whose sole purpose is evangelizing. The whole church has begun to pray and intercede. They are attacking us day and night with their prayer chains and fasting. The bombing and war are intense. They all seem to be aware that Christ will not come to reign unless the Gospel is preached in every nation and to people of all languages.'

'We are fighting continually, but we can't stop them. They just keep on advancing,' he continued in a trembling voice.

'What are we going to do?' roared Satan. 'All is lost! Thousands have been saved, and this last piece of news is the worst of all. He could come at any time. It will not be long, because with the vision that these people have, soon people of every tribe, language and nation will be reached with the Gospel. And then what will become of me? Woe is me!'

The responsibility of the Church

One day, as I was interceding, God gave me a vision. I found myself in a beautiful place. There was lush green grass, flowers and plants of all colours and shapes. I had never seen anything like it. I also saw a crowd of smiling and happy people who were enjoying that beautiful place. I thought I must be in heaven. But suddenly towards the back of the image that I could see, I noticed a very high fence that was impossible to climb over. I wondered what it was, so in my vision, I went closer to the fence and looked over it. To my surprise, everything on the other side was brown and arid, with no vegetation. I could also make out shadows, and as I looked closer, I realised that these were people who had been living for many years in this desert. Their clothes were worn, their hair dirty, and they were gasping for something to drink. Everyone was desperately staring at the oasis that was located on the side where I was standing, along with other believers. Some seemed to be holding out their hands for help, others were crawling, but all of them seemed to be asking for something. All I could make out were the following words: 'Help us! Give us some water, please!' They were trying to reach those of us who were on the other side, but there was no way we could cross the barrier, nor could they come over to us.

Then, all of a sudden, I sensed a voice telling me 'Tell my Church to take down every barrier, every fence, and all blocks that separate them from those who hunger and thirst, not for bread and water, but for God.' That is the responsibility of the Church.

Our responsibility is to ensure that the world gets to know Jesus Christ. If we want to win the lost, we need to get out and fight in enemy territory, because the world is under the control of the evil one. We know that we belong to God, and if we love people, we have to go into the devil's territory, into the world, to snatch the souls that Satan is holding captive in his claws. God has sent us to take back what the devil has stolen. But we must understand that we cannot enter the devil's territory empty handed, without the weapons required to win the battle.

Hardness of heart

Many times we make excuses by saying that people do not get converted because of the hardness of their hearts. But that is not the case.

I remember one time when I was in Europe, I got talking to a group of pastors. During the conversation, one of them commented, 'Evangelism is hard going here, because the people of this city are hard-hearted.' I didn't respond, but the words stayed with me.

We were staying in a beautiful place, near the sea. From the site of our campaign we could see some lovely properties. Some of them were mansions of three, four or five floors. I'm sure the people who lived there were upper class, with a lot of money. As I admired the beauty and looked at the view, God spoke to me, saying 'Carlos, go and knock on the door of one of those houses, and tell them you want to talk to them about me. They will listen to you.' Then I understood the passage of Scripture that says:

> How, then, can they call on the one they have not believed in? And how can they believe in the one of whom they have not heard? And how can they hear without someone preaching to them? (*Romans 10:14*)

If we are afraid to speak, we will never be able to evangelise the entire world.

I preached in that city for nine nights in a huge tent with a capacity for eight to nine thousand people. To the surprise of many, it was filled every night of the campaign. Those who had said we could not evangelize because of the hardness of people's hearts were able to watch around two thousand people come forward each evening, with their hands held high, to give their lives to Jesus.

The veiled Gospel

The task of evangelism depends on us, not on the people who need to hear it. 2 Corinthians 4:3-4 explains this as follows:

> And even if our gospel is veiled, it is veiled to those who are perishing. The god of this age has blinded the minds of unbelievers, so that they cannot see the light of the gospel that displays the glory of Christ, who is the image of God.

Why is the Gospel veiled? Because the god of this age, the thief, the usurper, has blinded the minds and the understanding of unbelievers so that they cannot see the light of the Gospel.

There is no such thing as a heart that is hard towards God. Instead, Satan uses a spirit of unbelief to blind people's minds and understanding. If people don't believe, it's because a spirit of unbelief is controlling them

So if our Gospel is veiled, and the god of this age has blinded the minds of unbelievers, what do we need to do to make people believe? We need to drive the god of this age out of the area, and tell him, 'Satan, spirit of unbelief, loose the minds!' When Satan lets go of the minds, the light of the Gospel can shine in people's lives.

I always enjoy going to preach in homes. When I am able, or when I am invited to pray for someone in their home, I preach to all the members of the family. If they do not receive Jesus into their hearts, I don't pray for healing. But if they do receive Him, I ask the Lord to do a miracle. I'm not some sort of faith healer. The first thing I always do is preach the Gospel. I have met all kinds of people. Once, when I was visiting a family, I began to speak about the Lord, and all the members of the family sat around me listening carefully. All except the grandmother, who stayed in the kitchen, from where she could hear what was going on. Everyone seemed to be agreeing with what I was sharing, except the grandmother, who kept coming out of the kitchen to interrupt me.

'You make people pay tithes.'

Surprised by her comments, that had nothing to do with what I had been relating, and trying not to lose the thread of what I was saying, I answered her: 'No, ma'am, it's not like that. Don't get me wrong,' and then I tried to explain the matter to her.

'I see,' she said and retreated back to the kitchen.

No sooner had I got back to what I wanted to say to those around me, who were all listening intently, than the grandmother appeared again from the kitchen.

'But you don't believe in Mary.'

Once again I explained to her that while we believe in Mary, and we love her, we don't venerate her, because she is not God. Jesus is the one we worship. By this time I was getting quite annoyed, because every time the family were ready to make a commitment to Jesus, she would interrupt me and stop what we were doing. So I decided to ask if I could use the bathroom. And what did I do there? I got down on my knees and took authority: 'Satan, spirit of unbelief, spirit of argument, loose the minds right now!' I kept praying like this for several minutes. The place was a bit cramped for doing spiritual warfare, and after a few minutes I could feel myself sweating. I came out of the bathroom red in the face, and the assembled group looked on amused as I retook my place in the lounge. This time, when the grandmother appeared, she took a seat beside me and said: 'Pastor, it's lovely that you could join us today. Please go on with what you were saying.'

At the end, the whole family accepted Jesus, including the grandmother.

Remember that our struggle is not against flesh and blood.

Our enemies are the principalities and powers.

We have power and authority in the name of Jesus, but Satan will only respect that authority when we exercise it. He no longer has rights over us, but he doesn't want to release that which he has held for so long without a struggle. We exercise authority as we stand in the authority of the name of Jesus, and command Satan to release the souls that he has kept captive, and which do not belong to him. Then the power struggle begins. We have victory in our hands, but the devil does not want to admit it, because he is a thief and a scoundrel. Don't give up, because he will fight to keep hold of the souls. That's why it's important to know what authority God has given us, and what weapons we have to fight with.

The works of Satan

In 1985 the entire city of Rosario was touched by the power of the Gospel. We saw thousands and thousands of people give their lives to Jesus. Most of the churches in the city were actively involved in the campaign. Denominational differences were laid aside, as everyone joined together in order to win the lost for Christ. God responded by doing amazing miracles.

But what I am about to relate happened ten years later, when I returned to Rosario to do another evangelism campaign. One day, after our team intercession time, I headed into the centre of the city to do some shopping. It was a day like any other; sunny, warm and the forecast was good.

Suddenly, as I walked along, I noticed litter flying around and the leaves on the trees starting to shake, as a strange wind began to blow. I could see blue sky above, so I couldn't understand why there was this sudden storm. But the violent wind kept blowing, and I realised that something unusual was happening.

Rosario is located in the Province of Santa Fe, to the north of the city of Buenos Aires. As I watched this strange weather,

I realized that the wind was coming from the south. The dark clouds were coming from the direction of Buenos Aires, and they were coming together at different heights directly above the city where we were doing our campaign. Within a few seconds, the clouds had completely covered the city, blocking out the sun, and bringing with them this strange wind.

As I surveyed the scene, I heard God's voice saying 'Carlos, what you seeing are legions of demons, coming from Buenos Aires to oppose the campaign.' The spiritual struggle was being made manifest before my eyes. I was watching the devil's preparations and schemes to ensure that the Gospel was not preached. I realised that the spiritual rulers of the territory of Rosario were being reinforced by others from the province of Buenos Aires.

Satan was getting ready to hinder the campaign in order to prevent thousands of souls from coming to the feet of Jesus. That is why I never get tired of saying that the Bible is very clear when it says that our struggle is not against flesh and blood, but against the principalities, against powers, against the rulers of the darkness of this age, against spiritual hosts of wickedness in the heavenly places.

This experience confirmed to me the importance of fighting, spiritual warfare and the opposition of the enemy to try to stop the advance of the Gospel.

Snatching souls from the devil's clutches

We cannot ask the Lord to do our work for us, and then sit around and wait for things to happen. He has granted us authority that we might use it to command the devil to loose the souls, in the name of Jesus.

As children of God, let us reclaim our city, and our nation for Christ, but let's realise that we need to fight for them. The devil will not give up anything without a fight. Satan will not give us anything. We'll have to fight for everything in the name of Jesus. Do we want the city? Then we have to command him 'Satan loose the city, in the name of Jesus!' This is the only way. How we pray will determine whether the powers and principalities will start to falter. Then we will see people running to the feet of Jesus. When the spiritual world starts to retreat in disarray, it doesn't matter who we are preaching to, their social status or culture, because they are no longer being controlled.

If you want to see your city transformed by the light of the Gospel, you need to take authority, and fight in prayer and intercession against the devil and his forces, against the spirit of unbelief, ordering him to loose the souls, in the name of Jesus. Then we can preach the Gospel, and people will respond.

When the pastors in a city join together to organise an evangelism campaign, all hell is let loose. The principality over the place, with all his powers and forces, starts to put obstacles in place to make sure it doesn't take place. What I told you at the start of this chapter makes this clear.

A city transformed by the power of God

In 1984, at the beginning of our ministry, we were preparing for a campaign in the city of Mar del Plata. We had planned that it would last fifteen days with the possibility of extending to twenty days.

When we arrived at this seaside resort on the coast of the province of Buenos Aires, we checked into a hotel located on the seafront. At that time, Mar del Plata was the most important tourist city on the Atlantic Coast of Argentina. Between two and three hundred thousand people used to visit each summer.

While one of my colleagues was filling in the forms in reception,

I went over to a large window to enjoy the view. Suddenly, a woman who had been leaning against one of the pillars which adorned the hotel lobby, walked rapidly towards me and grabbed me by the arm. 'Please tell me about Jesus,' she implored me.

I was quite taken aback, because I had never seen her in my life before. It was the first time that we were doing a campaign in this city, so she knew absolutely nothing about us or what we were doing there. So what was making her act in this strange way? We realised that the Holy Spirit was convicting her of her sins.

That very day she had contemplated suicide because she felt overwhelmed by the problems in her life, and unable to carry on. I didn't know her situation, but I could see the desperation in her face as she came over to ask me to tell her about Jesus. So I told her the Gospel, and with tears in her eyes, she accepted Jesus into her heart. She was the first person to get saved in that amazing campaign of 1984.

Still in a state of shock from what had just happened, I joined the others, and we went up to our rooms. We entered the room that we were sharing, and my colleague went over to the window overlooking the sea. I could tell from his reaction that he was receiving a vision, and he started to tell me what he could see. He was amazed to see three giants rising over the sea, as they tried to seize control of the city. But something like a huge invisible wall was stopping them. Around them were countless demons jumping on the water, bouncing against the huge wall that held them back. I was amazed by the vision, and it was quite a time before my colleague recovered.

Once the campaign started, we realised the significance of the vision. One of the special things about the campaign was that all the churches of the city were taking part: Mennonites, Brethren, Baptist, Christian Alliance, Pentecostals, Assembly of God, Missionary Movement of Christ, Salvation Army. All these denominations, which rarely come together, were working alongside each other, with the common goal of evangelizing the city of Mar del Plata.

Right from the start of the campaign, supernatural things began to happen: some people were falling down in the streets under the influence of the Holy Spirit, others were experiencing demonic manifestations in their homes. The miraculous was everywhere. When we realised the incredible move of God that was taking place, we decided to extend the meetings. After we had been preaching for forty-five nights, we had to move to the main football stadium for a further fifteen days, in order to accommodate all the people who wanted to attend.

In total, 83,054 people accepted Jesus as their Lord and Saviour during that huge campaign entitled '*Mar del Plata, Jesus Loves You!*' in 1984. The largest circulation national newspapers and magazines carried headlines like 'More people attend evangelical meeting than all theatres and events combined.' In the city stadium, the fans started to chant our campaign song, *The man of Galilee* during matches.

The miracles kept increasing; many had their dental cavities filled with gold sent from heaven. So what was behind this great move of God, and the supernatural outpouring of His grace? I put it down to, firstly, spiritual warfare and intercession, and secondly, the unity between the churches. We were able to see how the strong man was kept bound and could not enter the city.

This shows us clearly the power of intercession, and that what Jesus taught us is true: 'Father, may they be one, so that the world may believe.'

If we want to defeat the one who came to steal, kill and destroy, then we as the Church, as the body of Christ, cannot stop praying, interceding and doing spiritual warfare.

When the strong man loses his authority, when the prince is bound, when the rulers are thrown down, people begin to believe. Automatically, the god of this age loses his authority, he lets go of the minds of the people, and the Gospel shines out.

That's why our struggle is not against flesh and blood. The Church has power and authority, and we must use it.

Victory is in our hands

We need to get ready to look at the crowds and tell them, 'Jesus loves you!' God has compassion for our land and for our people. Let us not take a single step backwards, because we have already retreated too far. Satan has taken over the territory that we have left empty. We have abandoned the parks, the squares, the stadiums and the streets, allowing the devil to spread sin and suffering. Let us not give up any of the rights that we have as Christians.

God has given us the power to conquer the land. What we have seen and heard is nothing compared to what He wants to give us. The truths of God must be proclaimed in every direction, so that Satan quits his lying. May God's words no longer be kept within the walls of our buildings, and may His message overcome all barriers. The North, the South, the East and the West must hear the message of the Gospel.

We need to preach with courage and boldness, just like the early Christians, who often ended up in jail. God wants us to confront and fight against sin, rather than the sinner. And who is the one behind the sin? The one who came to steal, kill and destroy.

God has not changed. Jesus Christ is the same. Lord, enable us to preach your word with great boldness.

> Now, Lord, consider their threats and enable your servants to speak your word with great boldness. Stretch out your hand to heal and perform signs and wonders through the name of your holy servant Jesus. (*Acts 4:29-30*)

7

A Call to Spiritual Maturity

When I was young, and before I knew the Lord, my work was the most important thing in my life. I wanted my family to have a good standard of living and never to have to want for anything. And so by hard work and effort I built up a business in the city where I lived.

It began as a hardware store, but as the business grew and prospered, it specialised in the supply of tools and machinery to industry. Looking back over the years, I can see how the Lord has prospered my business to enable me to finance evangelism campaigns all over Argentina.

So whenever I was not away on a campaign, I would be working in the business, helping to move things forward. Some of my children would often come with me because there were always lots of exciting things going on. While I would be in the office, signing papers or having meetings, they would be running around the large premises, getting up to mischief. Their fun usually ended up with a mess in the area where they were playing. They especially enjoyed playing in the section that was filled with boxes of all kinds of screws, nuts, bolts, etc, each one labelled by their size and type. Their favourite game was for one of them to hop on one of the trolleys that was used for transporting loads around the store, while the others would push the trolley at high speed up and down the narrow aisles. This usually ended up with the trolley crashing into a wall of meticulously ordered boxes, which would come crashing down in a shower of screws, washers, nuts and bolts, which would end up scattered across the floor.

While this was great fun for my kids, the store assistant responsible for keeping the area tidy took a different view. The first thing that I would know about all this would be when one or more of my kids would traipse woefully into my office complaining that so-and-so had twisted their ear. The store employees would frequently have to chase my kids out of their area, or sometimes even drag them out!

But as my kids grew older, they started to take responsibility for different areas of the family business. When they were young they would have their hair pulled or their ears twisted, but once they grew up, they would start to give instruction to the employees and take responsibility for different areas. From the beginning, my children were the heirs of the business, but they did not have the maturity or the ability to exercise authority as the owners. However, once they reached adulthood, they put childish things behind them, and started to behave like the rightful owners and managers of the business.

What I have just related is a picture of what happens in our Christian lives. When we first accept Jesus as Lord, we are born again, and like new-born babies, we depend on others to care for us. Although all the blessings of God's Kingdom are available to us, we rely on others to help us receive them, because our own understanding is limited. Although we are heirs, in reality we don't act like it.

The Bible explains the situation like this:

> If you belong to Christ, then you are Abraham's seed, and heirs according to the promise.
>
> What I am saying is that as long as an heir is under age, he is no different from a slave, although he owns the whole estate. (*Galatians 3:29-4:1*)

There are areas of our Christian lives where we have not yet reached a sufficient level of maturity to exercise the authority that Jesus has given us. This is not what God desires. It might be many years since we were born again, but we realise that we are still acting like spiritual children. Although we are heirs and masters of all, we are living like slaves, and not experiencing the life of freedom that Christ offers.

One of the signs of spiritual immaturity in the life of a believer is that the person can't achieve the freedom required to live a life of victory. They live as slaves, and the circumstances that dominate their lives push them one way and then the other, preventing them from moving forward.

This spiritual immaturity can also be found in the church, which is the body of Christ. Although we should be taking charge of the spiritual world, we find ourselves getting distracted by childish things.

As I travel around the world preaching the wonderful message of salvation, I often come across churches distracted by unimportant matters, while pain and suffering are growing all around. Selfishness, pride, jealousy, envy, gossip, one person against another, accusations, unresolved conflicts, children of God who refuse to talk to one another, to meet together, to work together, or to forgive one another. Some think that their group is more numerous or better than others, while others feel that their group has fewer, and are looked down on. These different traditions, ways of thinking and ways of working divide and separate us.

These symptoms of spiritual immaturity present us with a challenge that we need to overcome. The time has come to lay aside the unimportant matters such childish arguments, and start to work together in love, as Jesus taught us.

The above passage from Galatians shows us a wonderful spiritual truth: although a child might be the heir and owner of the whole estate, it doesn't have the ability to exercise the authority that has been given to it. So the father waits until the right time, until he sees that the child has a sufficient level of maturity and experience. We can't remain at the level of spiritual children all our lives. We need to grow up and mature in the Lord, in order to exercise the authority that God has given us in Jesus.

In Him we have recovered the authority to overcome the devil, and to bring about change. The Church of Jesus has authority to be a fountain of blessing to reverse the destructive work of the enemy. This authority has been given to us; all that remains for us to do is to grow up in God, believe that He has given it to us, and start to exercise it. By doing this, we will see changes in our lives, cities and nations.

> So you are no longer a slave, but God's child; and since you are his child, God has made you also an heir. (*Galatians 4:7*)

All that I am relating is the product of over thirty years of ministry. It is not based on extensive research or reading around the subject. It is based on the reality of what I have experienced. God has taught us and helped us to live out each of the points expressed here. All these experiences help me to keep living according to what the Bible teaches. I know that these principles work and that they produce supernatural results by God's grace.

We believe that every biblical principle that God has given us in His Word is there to be believed and applied, rather than just understood. When we, as children of God, live according to what He has taught us, then these promises become realities in our lives.

The hour has come for the Church to reach maturity, to leave behind childish things, and to work together so that the glory of God is reflected among us, and by us.

We can no longer allow Satan to hurt and bother us. The time has come to put him in his place, the place that Jesus gave him. He has been defeated and the Church has authority over him. For us, Jesus has won a destiny of victory, but for our enemy, a destiny of failure. It is time to take our place in God. There is a world out there that is groaning, and which has more serious needs with every passing day. There is a world out there that is waiting for the sons of God to be revealed.

What will you do with what God has given you and for which Jesus gave up His life?

Appendix

Kill the evangelist
by *Pastor Hugo Alberto Basile*

In October 2006, we went to the Argentine city of Santa Fe to do an evangelism campaign, which was set to go on for many days. The Holy Spirit worked powerfully, doing signs, wonders and miracles, healing the sick, and setting free those oppressed by the devil. Hundreds of people were set free from spiritual bondage, trauma, emotional wounds, and the suffering caused by sin, and transformed into a new life of light and fullness of the Holy Spirit.

I especially remember the penultimate day of the campaign. The weather was perfect that evening, and thousands of people came to hear the Gospel in the Federal Park, which provided a perfect setting. The atmosphere was one of joy and celebration, as the evangelist gave a powerful message of new life and hope. Suddenly the peace was interrupted by the loud yells of an enormous man who was making his way to the front, pushing and growling at everyone in his way. He appeared to have a supernatural strength, on account of the legion of demons that controlled his mind and will, and which terrified and enthralled all those standing nearby. He came right up to the platform, and using his hands, raised the one and a half tonne structure on which the evangelist was standing, about 10 centimetres off the ground. Everyone who saw what was happening pushed back as they tried to get away from this terrifying spectacle.

The evangelist, perched atop the tilting platform, responded by taking authority in the name of Jesus. 'Satan, devil, I bind you in the name of Jesus Christ of Nazareth!' Immediately the legions of demons that controlled him were left immobile. Throughout the remainder of the message and the altar call, this enormous figure was left there immobilized.

When the time came for the prayers for deliverance, the evangelist rebuked all unclean spirits present, and the powerful man was instantly knocked to the ground, turning over several times in the process. Several volunteers were soon on the scene to assist him to the deliverance tent where he received ministry.

This man was possessed by Satan, but he needed Jesus. He needed the freedom that only Jesus can give. In the tent, several volunteers ministered to him with love, compassion, and the authority of Jesus. After he had understood his need for salvation and freedom, and repented of his sins, he confessed and renounced each one, breaking the agreements that he had made with the devil. The list was long: family curses which had held his life in bondage were broken; he was set free from agreements with practitioners of the occult; he renounced all hatred, roots of bitterness, all sexual sins, and all the things that bound him to Satan. After several hours of ministry, he was completely free.

Later the same evening, he came to see the evangelist, and with tears in his eyes, he asked forgiveness for what had happened that night. He was ashamed of what the devil had done with his life and how the devil had used him to do his work. He explained that earlier the same day, his mother, who was a priestess of Satan because of a covenant she had made with the devil, was given the clear command to 'Kill the evangelist.' However, what Satan had intended for evil, Jesus had transformed for good, for the glory of God, by salvation and freedom.

Hugo Alberto Basile
Pastor and member of the ministry of Carlos Annacondia,
Message of Salvation.

Campaign 1984 – *'Mar del plata Jesus loves you'*
by Pastor Omar Olier

In 1978 God spoke to me personally, telling me that he was going to give us the city of Mar del Plata. Although I didn't understand very much, in faith, I began to pray and fast once a week for the burden that the Lord had put on my heart. From my position on the staff of a local church, I failed to see any sign of what the Lord had told me was going to happen.

Year after year, God continued to confirm the word through dreams and visions given to other local Christians, in which He said He was going to do something big in the city of Mar del Plata. In response to this, we conducted evangelistic meetings, we kept fasting, and in faith preparing ourselves for the time when God would fulfil what He had promised.

One day, news reached us from the city of La Plata, close to Buenos Aires, of a man that God had raised up, and whom He was using in a tremendous way. We wanted to see if what they said was really happening. Perhaps this could be the man whom God would use to bring revival to our city. It was with a tremendous expectation that we travelled to the city of La Plata.

All that we saw at the campaign had a tremendous impact on us, particularly the way that the evangelism and ministry were done. We immediately began to make plans for the ministry of Carlos Annacondia to come to our city, but this did not prove easy, because one of the requirements of the ministry was that the campaign should be organised by a group of united churches. Many of the pastors in Mar del Plata knew nothing about the ministry, and many of those that did, didn't agree with it. Ours was a challenging task that required prayer and perseverance. But finally, on October 19th, 1984, the campaign entitled *Mar del Plata, Jesus loves you* with the evangelist Carlos Annacondia, started.

It was a great privilege to get to know Carlos Annacondia personally during the preparations for the event, and this was something foundational for me at the start of my own ministry. Through time spent with him and his family over meals, I came to realise that God is sovereign and does as He wants. Titles and qualifications are not important to Him. Here was a man who had an incredible burden for lost souls, that came from a tender heart that was intimately in touch with God. I had never seen anything like it. I was struck by his commitment, the authority he had for deliverance, and the incredible gift of faith for healing, which became apparent during the campaign. The most striking thing of all was that this was accompanied by a deep humility and a willingness to share with others all that he had received by God's grace. This really blessed me.

Carlos' friendship and ministry transformed my life. He passed on his ministry, and continues to do so, to those who are prepared to receive it and use it in the service of the Lord. Wherever he went, he passed on to others the same anointing.

This set him apart from any other evangelist that I had met up until that time. Evangelists used to come to our city, preach at a meeting, and after they left, any sign of revival would disappear. But Carlos was different.

Many pastors and Christian leaders discuss the work of God in their cities in terms of 'Before Annacondia's visit' and 'After Annacondia's visit.' Mar del Plata is no exception. At the start of my ministry back in 1978, I saw the city as a wheat field ready for harvest. But after 1984, I came to see things differently; the heads of the wheat stalks were no longer pointing upwards, but were pointing downwards, signifying their ripeness. All that remained to be done was to harvest and to prepare the barns for storing the grain. Those who go out onto the streets in obedience to God's commands to harvest will not return empty handed. And by God's grace, this is what we did. God responded, and was faithful.

The ministry of Carlos Annacondia, more than any other evangelist that I have ever known or studied, is an instrument of God to increase the growth rate of churches involved in their campaigns. Dr. Peter Wagner states, 'After more than twenty years of study of city-wide evangelism campaigns, I can say that no other ministry has produced such a steady stream of testimonies.' I can attest that this happened in the city of Mar del Plata.

I had never seen any other campaign evangelist confront demonic powers so strongly in public. The campaign meetings were filled with a tremendous power and anointing. The healings and miracles that occurred were like in the book of Acts. These had a tremendous effect on our city. Here are some of the testimonies:

- Rosa Colasanto, who lives in the city centre, was diagnosed with breast cancer a few months before the start of the campaign. At one of the meetings, she fell down under the power of the Holy Spirit, and the cancerous tumour disappeared miraculously. Thirty years later she is serving the Lord, and testifying to what He has done.

- Olga Cosmano, who lives in the Las Americas neighbourhood, received a miracle in her teeth. During one of the meetings, the whole of the inside of the upper arch was covered in a platinum-like substance.

- Norma Ramirez, from the Florencio Sánchez district, came to a meeting suffering from a tumour located between her bladder and urethra. This disappeared completely during the prayers for healing.

- Juliano Vilches, from the Libertad neighbourhood, was healed of epilepsy.

- Fausto Reinoso, aged nine, and completely deaf, recovered his hearing instantly.

- Angelica Momoli was healed of tuberculosis and asthma.

These are just a few of the countless testimonies of the power and love of God. Even pedestrians walking near the campaign site fell down under the power of the Holy Spirit.

The ministry of Carlos Annacondia added to our ongoing work of evangelism a new emphasis on spiritual warfare and deliverance, that we had not known up until that time. We learned to proclaim the Gospel, not only to people, but also to the spiritual jailers that hold them captive, ordering them to let them go in the name of Jesus.

At last I was able to see the fulfilment of God's promise to me. Not only were 83,054 souls entrusted to us, but we also received the city. Over the thirty years since the campaign we have been able to reap the fruits of perseverance and effort. Today the results are clear for all to see.

At the time of the campaign, there were twenty churches in the city. Today, there are more than two hundred. The harvest continues. We have a weekly meeting of the pastoral committee comprising fourteen members, and a monthly meeting with all the churches.

Over the last ten years we have been joined by pastors from neighbouring cities. We can declare that, even today, the work of salvation, healing and miracles goes on. But above all, we know the authority we have over the enemy, by which God gives us power to bind and loose and see the fall of the kingdom of darkness.

Omar Olier

Pastor, *God is Love Christian Center*,
Mar del Plata, Buenos Aires, Argentina

Testimonies

Restoration of a family

When his mother was fourteen years old she became pregnant through a relationship with an older man. When the man left, she wanted nothing to do with the child who was ruining her life. This was how Nestor's life began, so it's hardly surprising that he has no memories of love or happiness in his childhood. Soon after his fifth birthday, his mother moved in with another man, who turned out to be violent towards Nestor and his mother. This man also had a son, and he was continually favoured over Nestor, who felt like he had been abandoned for the second time in his life.

Nestor really suffered from the continual mistreatment at the hands of his step-father. The slightest thing would cause him to fly into a rage and drag Nestor across the room by the hair, or beat him about the head. The daily insults made him feel totally humiliated. During PE classes at school, he had to make excuses for the bruises on his leg, the result of beatings with the cable of the iron.

By the time he was thirteen, he was tired of so much violence and mistreatment, so one day he confronted his stepfather and threatened to cut off his head with a knife during the night. From that time on the beatings stopped, but his life did not get any better. He started to hang out on the streets with guys who were in their twenties or thirties, and with them he would get up to no good. Desperately searching for happiness and an escape from his sad past, he started to visit brothels and get involved in all kinds of perversion.

After some time, he was able to get a decent job and a steady girlfriend, but instead of feeling happy, he felt more and more depressed. The only way that he could face each day was by downing two litres of beer before going out to work.

Sometimes he would find himself asking, 'Where are you God?' Everyone around him seemed to have a normal family, something which for him was a pipe dream. Since he thought that his life had no future, one day he took the sad decision to end it. He climbed up onto a high bridge in the city of Olavarria where he lived. He could hear an inner voice telling him 'Throw yourself off! It's the only way you'll find peace.' But something stopped him, and he couldn't go through with it. He was often tempted to slash his wrists with one of the large knives he used in his work at a bakery.

One day his girlfriend, Monica, announced that she was pregnant. Nestor was only nineteen, but he was determined not to repeat the mistakes of his parents, and so they got married. But even though they did everything they could to make married life a success, they soon realized that history was repeating itself. The first two years of marriage were marred by arguments and violence. It seemed that the only solution was separation.

Monica was the last in a long line of brothers and sisters. She always sensed that her life was unplanned and unwanted, and for that reason she experienced rejection. The lack of love which she had experienced in childhood left her unable to offer any kind of affection towards others, her family included. At eighteen years of age, she was certainly not ready to be a wife and mother.

But one day, Monica's sister invited them both to a lunch at the evangelical church that she attended. At first, Nestor would have none of it, because he had always felt abandoned by God. But when his sister-in-law persisted in inviting him, he agreed to go with Monica. He recalls: 'What touched me was the deep love I saw between the people who were present. It was the first time in my life that I had experienced anything like this.'

Shortly afterwards, an evangelism campaign began in the neighbouring city of Azul. Their new friends at the church told Nestor and Monica that there would be miracles, healings and all kinds of amazing things. The two of them decided to go, thinking it was just an outing with some friends from the church.

They arrived at the campaign site to find a huge crowd singing joyful choruses with their arms raised in worship. They listened to Carlos Annacondia preaching about the love of Jesus, and then came the moment for the altar call. Nestor and Monica looked at each other as they considered how to respond. They both knew that if they did not go forward, then they would end up going their separate ways. This was their last chance. There was no alternative but to accept Jesus into their hearts. So taking each other by the hand, they went forward to give their lives to the Lord. They had decided to give God a chance to restore them and give them a fresh start.

Until that point, Nestor had always blamed others for the problems in his life. But now, for the first time, he admitted his mistakes. 'I don't remember much of the message. What I do remember is the evangelist saying "All your sins are forgiven! God does not remember them any more!" And I believed it. It was what I needed to hear.'

When the evangelist began to pray for deliverance, the two of them fell to the ground, and lay there for several minutes. The next thing they remember is hearing Carlos give a call to service: 'God has great plans for your life.' Nestor responded by dedicating his life to Jesus, so that He could do with it what He thought best. 'Lord, here I am. Please use me!'

'I was in floods of tears,' he remembers. He couldn't stop crying all the way home, with his wife by his side. The night that he accepted Jesus into his heart was the happiest moment of his life. For the first time ever, he felt a peace and a joy in his heart.

The visit to the campaign produced a complete about turn in Nestor's life. Step by step, God transformed his personal life and his marriage for the better. The change was immediate. He received a deep love for Jesus and a tremendous conviction of sin.

His wife was also strengthened in her faith as she watched the changes taking place in her husband's life. He had always been fascinated by martial arts, but from that moment on, he realised that God was not pleased with that, among many other things.

From that day on, despite the many challenges that they have faced together, Nestor and Monica have never given up serving the Lord. Over the last twenty-five years, they have continued to attend the same church where they first heard the message of the love of Jesus. They are now the pastors. They have three beautiful daughters, all professionals, who share the faith of their parents.

'For many years I believed that my life would be short and sad,' says Nestor 'But now I realise that brother Annacondia was right when he said "God has great plans for your life!"'

Healing from AIDS

During five long years, depression, abuse and the prognosis of death were my constant companions. There was no hope for me or the child that I was carrying. We were living in the early years of the AIDS epidemic, and understanding about the disease was poor.

I had seen a friend die of this terrible disease, which deprives a person of their senses one by one. I had seen the look of confusion on the faces of her children as they tried to understand why their mother had to die. For me there would be no more Christmases or New Years, and my son would never know the mum who loved him so much.

A friend once told me about the evangelism campaigns of the

Message of Salvation ministry, where many were healed and set free. Ever since, I had never stopped asking, 'Are there going to be any campaigns? When is there going to be another campaign?' Finally, my friend had some good news for me, and she agreed to take me along to a campaign that was happening in a suburb of Buenos Aires called Moreno.

I hardly had the strength to walk, but with my friend's help, we made it to the site of the campaign. When the time came for the altar call, I felt something propel me forward with the many others who gathered in front of the platform. During the prayers for healing, the evangelist placed his hands on my head, and I was instantly filled with an incredible peace. My mind became much clearer, and I knew something had happened.

A few days later, my wonderful son, Joel, was born. I'll never forget the incredible happiness I felt when the doctors told me that he did not have HIV; he was completely healthy. At least for him, there was a future of life and hope. I was still having to take higher and higher doses of medication to try and combat the effects of AIDS in my own body.

Some time later, I was invited to another campaign, this time a bit further away. But I made the journey, carrying my baby son in my arms, because I knew that only a miracle could save me. Even before getting off the bus that took us to the site, I could hear the choruses of faith and hope that the crowd were enthusiastically singing. Some were clapping, others had their hands held high in worship; many testified to what Jesus had done in their lives.

That night, the evangelist told the story of the blind man, Bartimaeus, who raised his voice to cry out for healing 'Jesus, Son of David, have mercy on me' (*Mark 10:47*). His cry was the same as mine, a cry that came from years spent in tears and groans. When the time came for the altar call, I heard the invitation, 'Come, Jesus is calling you!' I literally ran through the crowds in desperation, with my baby in my arms. I knelt and prayed with all my heart. Jesus heard my cry for healing from the disease that had put an end to my dreams. I knew that God had touched me.

I went back to see the doctors and they did extensive tests to see if I still had AIDS. But they could find no trace of the virus in my body. They can confirm that I have been completely healed. That was more than ten years ago, and in that time I have not needed any treatment. Low immunity and all the problems that go with that, now belong to the past.

What happened to me was not just something emotional. I am living the healing and restoring power of Jesus Christ. I never felt more fulfilled than I do now.

My husband and my oldest son have also experienced the power of God. Friends and neighbours, who witnessed my darkest days, have also come to receive Jesus Christ as Lord because of His amazing grace to me through salvation and healing.

Some time ago I was baptized, and I attend a church in the Ciudadela neighbourhood of Buenos Aires. I work on a daily radio programme, and give testimony to what Jesus has done in my life. Now it's the turn of others to ask, 'Sandra, are there going to be any campaigns? When is there going to be another campaign?'

Set free from childhood trauma

'One day you will serve the Lord.' These were the words that set off the turn of events that brought Jesus into Margarita's life. A street sweeper, who used to clean the road in front of her house, stopped her one day to give a her a message from Jesus: 'You are going to serve the Lord!' he said insistently. In her desperate state, this was something she found very hard to believe, and so she answered him with a mocking laugh. But this man was not deterred, and he repeated several times that the Lord had a plan for Margarita and that one day she would be a servant of God.

No one had ever told her that something good could come of her life. That's why she responded as did; she just couldn't believe it was true. For as long as she could remember, her life had been full of suffering and pain. She lived her childhood in the kind of home that no one would wish to grow up in. Together with her mother and sister, she was a victim of the destruction that drugs and alcohol wreak on a family. Only when their father was out of the house, could they relax, but they always had a foreboding of his return, because that's when their suffering would start. Margarita's mother, traumatized by the experiences their drunk and drugged father made them endure, used to try to hide the daughters. But with threats and blows, he would soon find the hiding place, and drag the little girls out to be insulted and abused.

For a girl of her age, Margarita had already gone through more than her fair share of suffering. She remembers hearing an insistent voice inside her that used to confuse and frighten her with the words 'Kill yourself. Kill yourself!' This voice that haunted her was so strong, and her suffering so great, that one day, as she was lying in her room, she set fire to the mattress, hoping to be trapped by the flames. But much to her regret, the fire-fighters arrived on time, and managed to put out the fire. Her childhood was the worst nightmare that anyone could imagine.

Margarita was five when her mother decided to escape the constant fear and anxiety, and taking the two girls away from the village of their birth, moved to another city in Mexico. It was a tremendous relief to be away from their violent father, but this was short lived, and the pain and suffering were soon to continue. Margarita's mother had to work all day to support her daughters. All day long, the girls were alone, locked into a small room, so that no one could harm them. Later their mother arranged for an aunt to stay with them and take care of them. What she didn't know was that the pain and suffering for the girls continued. The poor girls had to stay in the room while their aunt had sexual relations with the various men that used to visit the room.

Realising that she could not look after them, their mother took the girls back to their home village, and left them with their father. The only person who had appeared to love them was gone, and once again they were exposed to insults, abuse and suffering. Once again terror reigned in Margarita's life, as she became a victim once more of her father's advances. He never viewed her as his daughter, but as a woman to satisfy his desires.

After a time, when Margarita was fifteen, she was surprised when her mother returned to find them. She was no longer alone, but had formed another family, with a husband and newborn child. Trying to live all together as a family again was difficult for Margarita and her sister, because they didn't fit into this new home, and their mother only had time for the baby.

Once she reached the age of seventeen, Margarita thought that things would get better if she could start her own family. That was how she came to get married to a young lad, not out of love, but to try and escape an unhappy home and a history of anxiety and pain. But the chains that had bound her since childhood continued to hold her captive. Looking for a way of escape, they decided to move to the United States. But nothing changed. Once she realised that having her own husband and family did not change the reality of her situation, she went out into the street, with the same idea that had haunted her since childhood: taking her own life.

It was with this thought in mind that she bumped into a neighbour, who suggested something to her that seemed the answer to her problems. That was why she agreed to accompany him to what she thought at first was a church service. But as the meeting went on, she began to feel uneasy. Thankfully she was able to leave this occultic ritual before they were able to harm her.

Over the next few months she tried all kinds of things which promised solutions to her problems, such as parapsychologists and mediums. She made several further unsuccessful attempts to end her life. Finally, exhausted, she gave up all hope of ever finding an escape from her past. It was then that she recalled the words that the sweeper had given her: 'You are going to serve the Lord!' With tears of despair streaming down her face, Margarita got down on her knees in her room and began to pray 'Lord Jesus, if it is true that you exist, please come into my life! Change me. I need your love because so far no one else has been able to provide it! I don't want go on like this.'

At that moment, she felt the presence of God very strongly, and something inside her changed forever. She felt like a new person. When she saw her husband, she fell in love with him; he seemed different. She thought, 'What beautiful children God has given me! What a beautiful family I have!'

From that day on, the Lord began to restore her life: she and her family began to attend a church; God's love filled her home and many things changed. However, Margarita just couldn't get free from the past. The things that she had lived through were so strong that they never ceased to torment her. The memories produced so much distress. After two years of knowing the Lord and allowing him into her life, Margarita was invited to attend a church where two brothers from Argentina were going to pray for deliverance. At first, she thought that it wouldn't be good to go to the meeting, but then the Lord spoke to her and said 'I need you to be there. I have something for you.'

So, in obedience to the voice of God, she went along to the meeting. When the brothers began to teach about deliverance, Margarita experienced thoughts of rejection. 'I don't need this. God has already forgiven me.' But, despite her doubts, she asked for prayer to get free of the past and agreed to receive ministry. After renouncing all her sins, including the hatred and resentment she felt towards those who had harmed her, Margarita felt complete freedom.

Looking back on the experience several years later, Margarita commented, 'Now I understand what it takes to be free. I had to renounce, in the name of Jesus, all my sins of the past, the bitterness and hatred, and all impurity. Now I understand why the Bible says, "My people are destroyed from lack of knowledge" (*Hosea 4:6*). I am so grateful that the Lord led me and my husband to the place of deliverance. Now I am free for the glory of God. Jesus restored my life, and my family, and now we are serving Him together! Glory to God! The road sweeper's word to me has been fulfilled!'

☙